Table of Contents

D0556548

How to Do a Demo Quality
RECORDING
in Your Bedroom
2nd EDITION

tech
master
SERIES

By Peter Lawrence Alexander
with Jeff Sheridan
Illustrated by Caroline J. Whitear

HAL•LEONARD®
CORPORATION

7777 W. BLUEMOUND RD. P.O. BOX 13819 MILWAUKEE, WI 53213

ISBN 0-634-02615-1

HAL•LEONARD®
CORPORATION
7777 W. BLUEMOUND RD. P.O. BOX 13819 MILWAUKEE, WI 53213

Visit Hal Leonard Online at
www.halleonard.com

Acknowledgments & Bibliography

A few years ago, all "personal recording" (as it was called then) was done on a four-track cassette player. If you had extra money, you had a four-track reel-to-reel (whoa!). If you were studio driven or just really ambitious, you jumped from the four-track cassette recorder to possibly the new 8-track on 1/4" tape or 16-track on 1/2" tape players. To add effects, you'd get outside boxes, cables, ad infinitum. The point is, the central piece for recording for the masses was a four-track cassette recorder and the medium of recording was tape.

Today, that's completely changed.

The main medium of recording is not tape, but digital hard drives in either a computer or a computerized digital recorder. Few think of cleaning tape heads as much as they do defragmenting their hard drives. Instead of head alignment, we're concerned about latency and syncing.

Effects are included in the software, and in most cases with hardware digital recorders. You can buy more effects called plug-ins and you can get a whole suite of them (from Arboretum, TC Works or Waves) for what you'd spend on a single effects box. And they're programmable. And you can save the effects on your hard drive. Or if you have a digital recorder like the Roland VS-1880, you can get effects expansion boards that come with, literally, 1000 different effects ready to go.

In the privacy of your home and with sufficient budget, you can literally have a world class project recording studio capable of producing first class work, provided you have the requisite skills to go with it.

Never before have the options, complexities and learning curve been so numerous and so steep to simply record a basic song.

Nonetheless, certain key principles to the learning curve still apply, and I've focused on those in this present edition, but not without help.

I was guided in many areas by John Woram's *The Recording Studio Handbook*, originally published by Elar. Though out of print for just shy of two decades, it still remains a standard, with principles as valid today as in 1981 when it was first published. I've referred to this work often, sometimes by citing the book's title, other times by saying, John Woram reports..."

For guitar, I have learned greatly from Jon Chappell's *The Recording Guitarist*. If you're a guitarist or need to record guitars, it should be in your library. As should *The Musician's Guide to Recording Acoustic Guitar* by Dallan Beck of Musician's Institute. We greatly profited from Loren Alldrin's practical experience in *The Home Studio Guide to Microphones*, and we were enlightened by the many useful recording articles found online at *Sound on Sound Magazine* (**www.sospubs.co.uk**). You will be, too.

Our thanks to Lee Watkins at Hosa for his insight on cables and exposition on audio patch bays. The tech's at Peavey were among the best, if not the best we spoke to, answering both phone and questions quickly, efficiently and with very good humor. Their web site, **www.peavey.com**, is a treasure trove of helpful buyers data and you're well advised to spend time there.

Michelle Kohler and staff at Shure worked with us on the Shure Gallery of Microphone Positions. They, too, have one of the top web sites around for practical information and training. The basis of our Gallery came from their online PDFs. They are not only masters of making top quality mics, but an equal rarity, masters at showing you how to use them. This book is what it is because of their participation.

Our illustrations for the Shure Gallery came alive because of contributions from California Technology in Sacramento, and Caligari Corporation. Our 3D models came courtesy of 3D Cafe (**www.3dcafe.com**).

Some of the teaching in this work came from the *Hit Sound Recording Course* I published 10 years ago, which I produced with Bill Gibson. Bill moved on to write the *Audio Pro Home Recording Course* published by my colleague Mike Lawson at Mix Books. His success is well earned and my blessings and heartfelt appreciation go out to the Gibson family.

Jeff Sheridan of Soundworks Studios looked over my shoulder throughout this book. He is a team player par excellence and we are glad to have him as part of our teaching family. Any mistakes in this book fall onto my shoulders, no one else's.

Finally, there are not enough words in the dictionary of any language to express what my heart feels towards my wife, Caroline, who created every drawing including the superb 3D graphics in the Shure Gallery Collection. She is, in every sense of the full definition of the word, a partner. And the demonstration of her partnership is over 200 illustrations all drawn without a single word of complaint. I am honored to be her husband.

Peter Lawrence Alexander

Los Angeles, California

Summer 2001

Biography

Peter Alexander is the author of over 50 works, including: *How MIDI Works 99*, *How MIDI Works* 6th Edition, *Basic Cakewalk*, *Basic Cubase 32 5.0*, *Basic Emagic Logic*, the *Revised Rimsky-Korsakov's Principles of Orchestration*, *Counterpoint* by Fux, the *Applied Professional Harmony* series, *Electronic Arranging and Orchestration*, and many others.

Peter is a graduate of both the Richard Bland College of the College of William and Mary where he earned his A.A. Degree as a math minor, and the Berklee College of Music in Boston, MA, where he graduated with his B.A. in Music Composition. He is the most published graduate of Berklee to date. While at Berklee, he studied counterpoint and harmony privately with Dr. Hugo Norden of Boston University.

After graduation, Peter spent 10 years in the ad agency business working as a VP of Marketing & Media. His accounts included Pepsi, McDonald's, CBS and others. During this period, he licensed from Time Magazine, their zip quintile concept of marketing and applying it to radio ratings, discovered geodemographic patterns of listening that could be applied to creating more precise product distribution plans, more effective media planning and buying by matching product profiles to other zip media profiles, radio station profiles, boosting radio ratings, plotting artist concert tours by specific zip code areas within an individual Nielsen TV market, and overall, how people use music.

In 1980, he moved to Los Angeles where he soon formed Alexander Publishing, which specialized in creating easy-to-use tutorials for music technology products and music in general. He studied orchestration privately with the Pulitzer Prize nominated composer, Albert Harris. Later, he became the late Henry Mancini's private computer tech until Mr. Mancini's passing.

He has evolved Alexander Publishing into Alexander University Inc., which now both publishes texts under the Alexander Publishing name and runs an online school with both accredited and non-accredited classes in music and music technology.

As a producer/composer, he has a number of works debuting throughout 2001-2002 including: *Journey to the Third Heaven, Psalms of Ascent, The Unfaithful Wife: The Story of Hosea and Gomer; Hannah's Tale*, and *Mary & Joseph; The Untold Story.*

Preface
My First Recording Session:
A History

The first time I entered a studio, I arrived as Toscanini (to conduct the session) and left as the Boob of Boston. I was brought in to conduct the session because I had a good reputation as a conductor. When blended with the headphones, my tortoise shell glasses projected the image of "in control." Furtwangler had nothing on me.

On this day, I discovered many, many lessons, the chief of which was that being able to write good music and conduct it to pull out the best from the musicians were one set of skills. Knowing how to do it in a recording studio was the third set, and the one I had not been taught in college, since composition majors weren't given recording courses.

When I first arrived with the scores, I was told I could wait in the control room. Growing up, that was usually the dining room where my mother and father would lecture me. So just hearing those words made me apprehensive. After a few wrong turns, me and my tortoise shells arrived in a quiet lit room reminding me of the CIC (combat information center) of a Navy destroyer or carrier. There was this long rectangle thing with lots of sliders and knobs. There were two black boxes with black mesh screens angled in each corner. Off to the left were a couple of recorders with 2" tape. My mind began to wonder. Was this a recording studio, or a SETI (Search for Extra Terrestrial Intelligence) installation?

Well, I figured it had to be a studio because of the big pane glass window that overlooked a wood floor vaguely resembling my high school's basketball court. There were music stands and chairs and a big piano out there, too. So I figured I was in the right place.

The control room was small and air conditioned. I sat for a while and no one showed up. Before long, I dozed off. A few minutes later, I heard the whooooosh BLUNK of the control door opening and closing. In walked the engineer with long hair, a tattoo on his right forearm, and a grunt.

"Are you session @#$%^&?" he asked.

"Uh...."

"Yeah. That's you. Let's do set up."

The Bible says, "Even a fool who keeps his mouth shut appears wise." So I kept my mouth shut and watched. Out came the music stands. Then came long, thick black cables coiled up like a cowboy rope. These were followed by boom stands and mics.

He looked up. "What kinda mics ya want? We got Shures (wow, a mic made from a deodorant can?) and we got Neumanns."

"Uh..."

"Jingle session?"

"Yeah."

"Shures."

"Right," I said with contemplative authority. So he returned the mics he had brought out into the inner conclaves of the studio and came back with the announced Shure's. They looked pretty much like what he brought out originally. This brought relief to a spirit now being troubled. "Was I supposed to know what a Shure was? And if so, who was supposed to tell me? And where did I find out that kind of thing? And who's Neumann anyway?"

About 20 minutes later, the first part of the ritual known as *set up* was concluded. We now went back into the control room to that rectangular obelisk he called a *mixing board*. I watched him punch lots of buttons and turn all kinds of knobs. What was he doing and why? I suddenly felt very intimidated.

Before long, the musicians came and we headed towards more familiar ground - music. We'd record the band first then the singers. I passed out parts, put my score on the stand, counted off, and we were taping. After the first pass, I walked into the control room and listened.

That's when I discovered the black boxes in the corner were monitors (another name for speakers). As I sat and listened, I was suddenly being hit with a set of questions I didn't know how to answer. What was my opinion of the balance? Did I like how he had panned the band? Should we EQ the bass drum more?

I was absolutely lost! I finished the session and fearfully walked back into the control room to begin doing the mix. That word I actually figured out by myself. But it was small comfort, because suddenly I was expected to help shape and approve a sound on tape to be aired on radio and television. Fortunately for me, the person who booked the session was there and had had a lot of time in the studio, both professional and at home where he recorded his songs and him singing them on a device called a Portastudio. I stayed until the entire session was over. But I was lost. I didn't know how to render a good opinion about how something should sound because I had never recorded before. They talked about reverb, echoes and plates. Plates? What did a plate have to do with recording? Isn't that what I ate off of?

By the time it was over, I felt pretty useless. Both I and the person who had booked me had come to the studio with two different sets of skills. In writing, arranging, composing and conducting I was the superior. But when it came to getting that sound into a reproducible medium that could be heard over and over again, I was the inferior. I learned quickly that recording, like music, is its own craft.

Years later, I was in the studio with Henry Mancini while he was conducting the score to *Ghost Dad* starring Bill Cosby. I closed my eyes, bent my head and listened. My ears affirmed that I had learned my orchestration craft to the place where I could point out and identify each orchestral device Hank had used. When the cue was over, I walked into the control room and listened. There, a transformation had taken place, one more severe than any jingle session I had every conducted. The aural experience separated by the wall and a few feet was astonishing. It was, truly, magic.

Suddenly, what had been so clear to me in the studio was lost in the magic of what happened from the studio to the tape with reverb.

It was a short, but incredible journey.

In this book, I take you on journey that starts, blessedly, at the beginning. It assumes that your starting point is a blank wall. That said, we'll have a beginning that's far earlier than most recording books. If there's any assumption, it's that your first experience in learning how to professionally record will either be at home or within a school program.

This book also takes into account that if you have a computer with a Soundblaster card, then you can either purchase software for under $100 US or download software from the Internet that lets you turn your computer into a digital recorder. You can even start learning with the mini-microphone that came with your computer. And depending on the program and how your computer is set up, you can record from 8-16 digital audio tracks and apply effects to them (Micrologic, Pro Tools Free, Cubasis, and Cakewalk Home Studio). With this starting point, your computer doubles as recorder and mixing board, and your desk or home office, well, that's your control room.

In reading this book, please understand that I don't write as a recording engineer. I'm a producer/composer in Los Angeles who mixes his own projects, then when budgets permit, brings in a professional engineer to polish the mix. Thus, my writing approach for this book is that of a reporter. This means that you have before you a highly readable book about producing music. I've kept technical terms to a minimum, only bringing them in when absolutely needed.

I've designed this book to be a guide, a resource you'll come back to many times. By the time you've completed this book, you'll know what a studio is and the procedures for creating a productive recording session.

Realize that once sound is on tape or digitized within a digital recorder, you can now ask and answer a different question, "How do I want it to sound?"

This question alone has many tools and software programs available that empower you with many options for many answers. You'll learn some of them in this book.

Over the years, I've been in lots of recording sessions in Los Angeles. My best teacher was Hank Mancini. Hank considered himself responsible for all issues of the recording session. The first person in the studio (besides me at the coffee urns and donut trays) was Hank. He watched how every chair and mic boom was placed. His recording engineer was hand-picked (Bobby Hernandez). Hank had a team, and every person who was there was there for a reason.

One of the best examples of Hank's craft in this area can be heard by comparing a score he wrote that was recorded on two albums. One was produced by Hank (*Mancini in Surround*), the other by Erich Kunzel and the Cincinnati Pops (*Mancini's Greatest Hits*). The cut is called *Arctic Whale Hunt* and the difference between the two recordings is subtle, but clear.

This brings us to a simple lesson. Much about recording is learned by observation and experimentation. Most of us are like Hank, songwriters/composers who record, and most often, produce our own works.

So again, the need arises for a technical simplicity that admits us to the language of recording, the tools of recording, and the process of learning to record, mix and burn your own CD. From that point forward, nearly all recording instruction is about equipment operations and experimenting with the various applications.

As I write this book, I'm also doing a dramatic score that requires a huge pipe organ with pipes made of gold playing in a dark underground cavernous chamber. What does an organ with gold pipes sound like? No one knows. But as the composer, it's up to me to create the solution! This is where recording and sound design add to the composer's craft of expression by becoming part of the composition. And as I learned so long ago, and continue to learn, and trust that you'll learn, it ain't just the notes.

Peter Lawrence Alexander

Los Angeles, California

Summer 2001

Introduction: What About Recording You'll Learn in This Book

This book is the text reference material for the Alexander University class called *Recording 101, Introduction to Recording*. Here I teach a very simple concept that has direct application for how you learn recording today in this technological age in which we live for the early 21st Century.

Definition ->Operations -> Implementation ->Skill

I call this the *Four-Part Learning Path*. It describes the learning process of how to develop artistic skill when using technology to express the art within. First you define the single task(s) that lead up to what you want to do. Then you learn how to operate the parts of the software or equipment (or both!) to do those tasks. Next, you continuously implement what you've learned from which comes skill.

How to Do a Demo Quality Recording in Your Bedroom (2nd Ed.) occupies a specific position in the *Four-Part Learning Path* and that's to teach the steps for live recording, with coverage of sequenced recording, whether you're doing it at home or in a studo.

To record live requires understanding

■ What a studio is

■ The equipment in the studio

■ Application to a home studio

■ Steps to quickly learning the signal flow in a mixing board (analog, digital, virtual)

■ Connectors and cables

■ Connections to the things that connect to a mixing board

■ Connecting those things to the mixing board

■ Mics

■ How to record those things into your recorder, analog or digital, using one and two mics only

For completion, I've touched on panning, effects, and some mixing. Thus the primary focus of this book is about recording sound to tape or hard disk with basics of shaping the sound with reverb and effects.

Also covered is how to connect PC digital audio workstations to the mixing board.

Once you've completed this work, the next steps are going thorugh *Recording and Reverb*, *The Effects Class*, followed by *EQ and the Final Mix*. All three classes are by award winning engineer, Jeff Sheridan.

If you're using MIDI equipment and any sequencing/digital audio program to do your work, you should go through *How MIDI Works 6th Ed.*, followed by our titles on *Cakewalk Sonar, Cubase 32 5.0* or *Emagic Logic 5.0*. Here I go into detail on MIDI recording, editing, mixing with fundamentals of how to record and do a basic mix in digital audio.

Expectations on learning to record

There are six key factors that affect your learning to record:

1. That learning to record comes from experimentation; there are no canned answers

2. That the quality of your recording is considerably affected by the room you record in and the noises inside and outside that room

3. That the quality of your recording is considerably affected by the quality of the mic you use. The better the mic you can use, the better results you're going to get

4. That the quality of your recording is directly affected by the quality of the equipment you record on and the effects you use

5. That the quality of your recording is directly affected by the quality of the musicians and singers performing your work

6. The experience and caliber of the engineer doing the recording, the mix and the final mastering

The story is told in Los Angeles about a group of Japanese engineers who wanted to absolutely recreate the sound of a famous American rock artist in their studio in Japan. The engineers came over and purchased exactly what the musician was using - amps, mixing board, mics, the works. Then they measured everything. How far was the mic from the amp? How far from the wall was the amp? And on and on. When they got back to Japan, they were elated and eagerly set up the studio based on the scientific assumptions they had deployed. Imagine their chagrin upon discovering that even though they duplicated the conditions exactly, the sound was still different. It simply wasn't the same as the musician had gotten from his studio.

Key Lesson - all of these are highly subjective issues outside the control of science and how-to books.

The one posible exception is the so-called MIDI project studio where everything is recorded digitally with no live recording done. Here the rules change because you're recording a sampled instrument into a hard disk system in which you'll create a room sound. Here, you can recreate a certain sound provided you have the same exact equipment, effects (and the exact effects setting used on the song) and the same synths and samplers. But even here some things will change depending on the size and quality room you work in and your monitors. It may sound exactly the same way when you record it, but if your listening conditions aren't exactly the same, it *will* sound different.

No experts required

This doesn't mean you have to be an expert or have ideal conditions to get your music to CD. Far from it. One of our Alexander University students has recorded four (!) CDs all of which hit the Top 10 for the New Age music list. What got him there was the commitment to finish and use the skills he had to the best of his ability. The Nike slogan, *Just Do It,* applies to music, too, and not just sports.

Equipment needed to learn

To learn recording, you need (at minimum):

1. A mic

2. A recorder

3. Tape or disk space for the recorder

4. A cassette deck to play back your music, or a CD burner in your computer so you can hear your music on CD

5. A musician with a musical instrument

6. A vocalist

7. A sense of experimentation

8. Your ears

9. A willingness to learn and above all, to self-correct by learning from your mistakes.

If you have just this much, you can begin learning.

Conclusion

Because I'm a composer who records and mixes in what's called a project studio, I've taken a reporter's approach in this current edition. In so doing, I've learned a key lesson: there are no canned answers, only starting points from which you learn through experimentation as you go.

So sit back, and enjoy the journey.

How a Major Studio Is Organized

Every major studio has three component parts. These are the control room, the actual studio where recording takes place, and a permanent isolation chamber/vocal booth, or as in the case at the older Warner Brothers studio in Burbank, California (now the Turner Studios), a portable chamber brought onto the main floor of the studio.

Within the studio

Within the studio will be the mic stands, mics, musicians, musical equipment, music stands, baggage, equipment containers, often a grand piano, cabling. And with certain violinists, the Wall Street Journal.

In a film scoring session, you'll often find the copyist and librarian, the music editor and, if at the last minute, orchestrators writing frantically. At Sony MGM for scoring sessions, caterers bring in large coffee urns (regular and decaf) plus one for hot tea, and often a tray of pastries.

All of these "objects" go into the ambiance of the recordings.

The studio itself

The physical size of the studio determines the kinds of recording projects it can do. Some studios are small and designed to handle voice-over work only. Here, you can only fit a few people. Others are larger and can handle a rock band. Still others can handle a symphony and chorus combined.

To help visualize this, I've taken the dimensions of three main studios and drawn them close to scale for you in a giant rectangular cube. This serves two purposes. First, you'll get to visualize just how big a studio needs to be for specific recording purposes. Second, to set your expectations about what you can expect from recording "live" at home in a non-recording environment. In the diagrams, look at the mic boom stand. From the floor to the tip is 10 feet.

Studio A

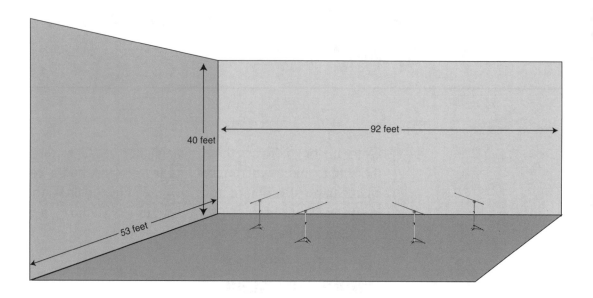

This studio can handle a full symphony orchestra plus a full chorus. With your imagination, fill in 80 players, full percussion, harp, conductor, music stands, people, pocket books, jackets, newspapers, etc. All of these objects go into the ambience of the room in a phenomenon called *room noise*. For editing later on, a wise engineer rolls tape long enough to capture the sound of the room. This way if changes have to be made, the room ambience isn't lost and consistency within the recording is maintained. For sports fans, the length of this room is only two feet longer then the distance from home plate to first base.

Studio B

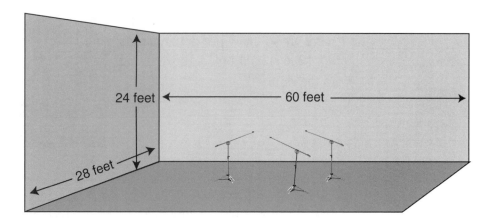

This is another good sized studio. The length of this room is the distance from home plate to the pitcher's mound. Or for football fans, 20 yards. It can handle smaller scoring sessions with a small orchestra or ensemble, live rock band, and so on.

Studio C

This studio is much smaller than the others. It can handle about a dozen or so musicians. Although this may seem at first to be a silly observation, note that room size determines the purpose of what you do in the room. Also remember that these are cutaways of pure blocks. The actual studios these were modeled after contain

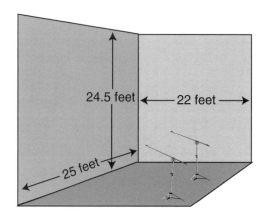

acoustic treatments, wood floors, and soundproofing. They're specifically built to record in.

Recording at home

Average room size for apartments or homes is 9 x 12 (which is why there are so many pre-cut area rugs 9 x 12 in size). Look at the drawing to the right:

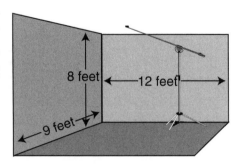

Notice that the average room height is 8 feet, but in the smallest studio we saw, it's three times as much. To make my teaching point, I have the boom mic literally going through the roof!

What this says in a very non-technical way, is that a recording studio has room for the sound.

And!

You're not going to record a rock group in a room 9 x 12! This means that your recording procedures, by the nature of recording in a non-recording environment, have to be different than if you were recording live in a studio. So let's look at how a typical home or apartment might layout for recording.

My "hall" studio

Now look at this "hall studio" layout. This is very typical of many homes and apartments (not drawn to scale).

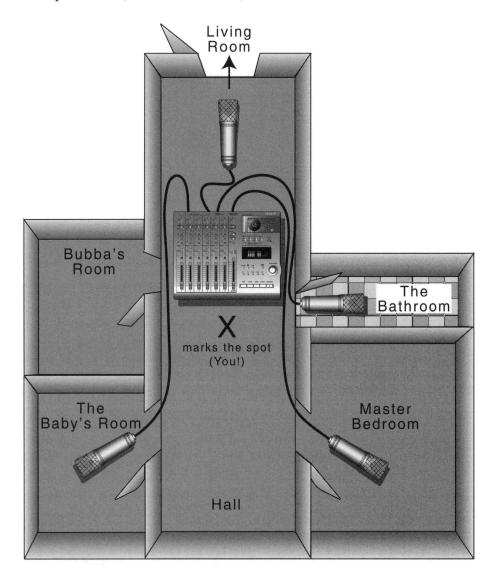

Here, the bathroom is used as a reverb room. Mics are running to the master bedroom, the baby's room, and one is snaking its way towards the living room. If the control room is in the hallway, how do you record everyone at once so that they're playing together? You can easily solve that problem if your dining room happens to be as large as a ballroom. But if it's not, then you have a serious logistical issue on your hands. Then there's the issue of furniture, like beds, chest of drawers, bureaus, diaper pails, windows, noise outside windows, drapes, and so on. If you have an extremely understanding family, you can move all the furniture out of the rooms to get a better sound. However, most families aren't that understanding.

The teaching point here is that the procedures for how you will record in a pro studio are drastically different from how you'll record in your home. Unless you have one incredibly huge home, you're going to find one room to do the work in, find the best place to record in that room, then record one musician and vocalist at a time. If you're recording in a MIDI project studio, that won't be an issue until you decide to record live.

Key home recording points

1. An engineer working in a studio, learns what the room sounds like and what to expect. Over time, he develops experience of how to set things up. For example, in Los Angeles, the main studios for orchestral recording are Sony MGM, Warner Brothers (now Turner Studios), Universal, and 20th Century Fox. Each of the four studios has a completely different sound and feel to them. Over time, you learn the room's sound and how to work the room. The difference in set ups, for example, between Warner Bros/Turner and Sony MGM, is based on the room. Certain rooms just have that certain something.

2. In a home or apartment, you're working around home acoustics, rugs, neighbors (with loud boom boxes),children, traffic, etc. You're shielded from all of these in the studio, but at home, these become workarounds you have to compensate for.

With a studio, you have a place to record. In your home, you're looking for the right spot. And that only comes by trial and success.

You *can* get a great recording at home

Don't misunderstand. You *can* get a great recording at home. But to do so first requires understanding how to operate the equipment/software and developing your ear to the place that you recognize when you have a good sound.

Your priorities are to get the operations down first, learn how to record, then begin refining by experimenting to find a good sound.

How technology helps

Units like the Roland BR-8, VS1680 or 1880, have effects features in them that permit you to record a sound dry (no effects). Then with reverb, effects, amp modeling, mic modeling etc., you can create both the room sound and the instrument sound within the system. Below is an amp modeling program called Revalver. With Revalver you can run your audio or guitar part through a specific virtual amp model, then apply the effects chain to create your guitar sound. All within the computer.

A key expectation setter

Every time you find a software program that gives you these options, your learning curve increases to learn how to operate the program, what it sounds like, and how to alter it for your needs. Also, it's equally realistic that your system spec may need to be upgraded to handle the extra load on the processor.

Effects within the programs

Let's look at Platinum Reverb from Emagic Logic. This is an excellent sounding reverb. Look below for three sliders labeled Room Size, Room Shape and Stereo Base. Logic comes with seven different room shapes built into the software. Now remember the studio layouts we looked at earlier. They were all rectangles. That's because unless otherwise so designed,

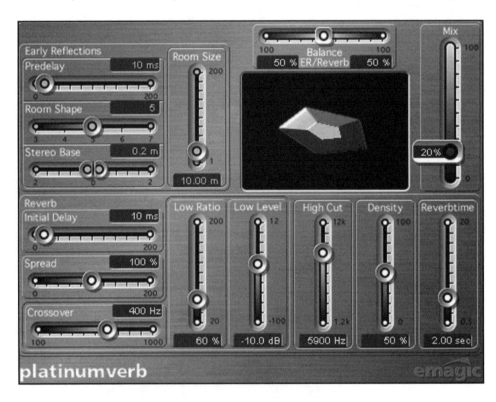

studios are rectangles! The acoustic treatment in the room does the altering. We also noted wall length. So where the slider is labeled Room Size, it's really the distance between walls from corner to corner. Being a European program, the wall measurements are in meters (m). So to get a concert hall large enough for a symphony (as we learned earlier) we could in theory set the Room Size for 30 meters (a little over 90 feet). Understand that this doesn't mean you just got Carnegie Hall for your strings! But it does say that nearly all of the software programs come with very flexible feature rich effects that can help you compensate for not being in The World's Greatest Studio.

The Room Simulator

Found in Samplitude 2496, the Room Simulator is a very interesting effect. Here you take the recorded sound of a room, import it into Samplitude, edit it, then instead of using what we call real time effects, place your music within that simulated room. Again, don't consider that a quick fix. It's a starting point from which you have to develop the sound of the space.

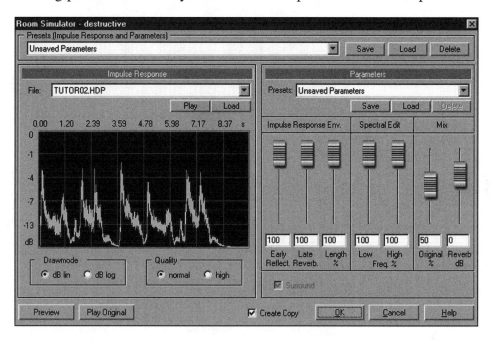

Free Filter by Steinberg

Free Filter, like it's cousin in Samplitude, lets you play in a recording, analyze the EQ that was used, and then lets you apply that EQ curve to your own recording.

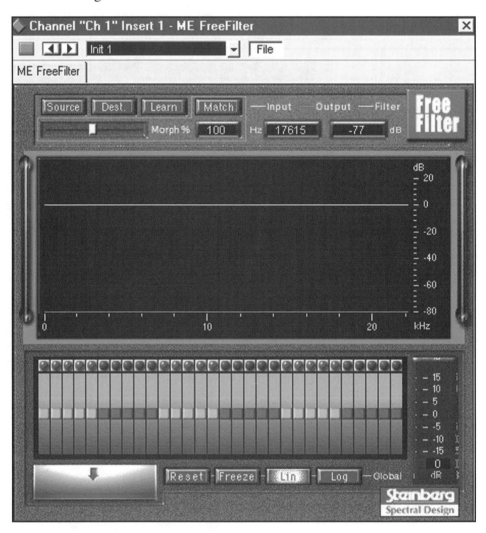

Note

Again, these are potential solutions, all of which must be learned before they can be effectively applied (no pun intended).

The Control Room

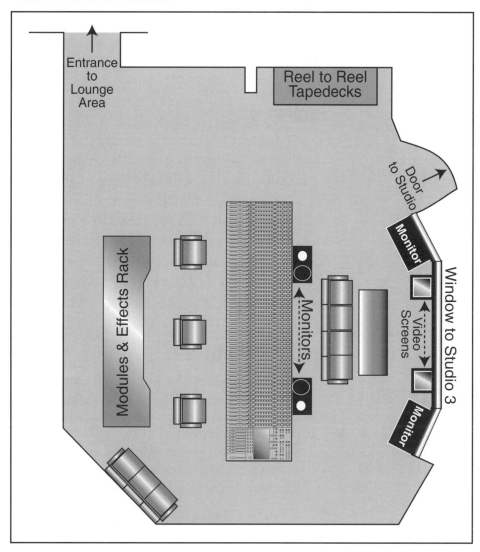

The control room has a glass window that lets you face what's happening inside the studio. Within the control room are the mixing board, the recorders, effects, patch bays and monitors. Effects are often placed in wooden cabinets directly behind the mixing console. A back cabinet door is opened for servicing. Along the walls can be other effects racks, and recorders, either hard disk or tape. There can be two - three chairs behind the mixing board (also called the recording console). In front of the console can be a couch, lounge chairs, and a coffee table plus phone. Control rooms have a very generic look about them. What you see in the diagram above is fairly common. The board featured is a Mackie 32-8 bus board with side car.

Isolation chamber/Vocal booth

Again, sometimes these are portable, other times permanent. Their purpose is to record a soloist(s) or vocalist(s) separate from the main ensemble. This permits a discrete direct recording that doesn't "leak" into other tracks.

Summary

In the home environment, the room in which you record doubles initially as both control room and studio. Except by luck or extreme wealth, it's not acoustically treated, and it isn't going to give you the same sound as actually recording in a studio. However, with experimentation and experience, you'll learn to find the sweet spots in a room and record there. The software or hardware that you use will often contain effects and features enabling you to compensate for recording in your home, with the understanding that the effect used for compensating has its own learning curve and unique sound.

Application to you

1. The computer, the Roland VS unit or the 4-track represents the control room. It contains the mixing board (console) and the digital recorder, and sometimes the effects.

2. Recording often takes place in the same room as where you have your equipment, unless you're able to run cables from the recorder to other rooms in your home or apartment.

3. Unless you construct an isolation chamber or vocal booth, it's common for the vocal booth to be (honest) your bathroom where towels are moved around to control room reflections (natural reverb).

STOP!

1. WHAT kind of music are you recording?

2. WHERE are you recording it?

3. HOW much space do you have to record including ceiling height?

4. WHO are the musicians or vocalists to be involved?

2 The Digital Audio Production Studio

Not displayed in our studio examples was the digital audio production studio. This is a hybrid studio that doubles as a studio/control center. All projects are handled digitally. If an artist is needed, they're brought in and recorded independently either in the studio/control room or in a separate studio. In the case of hip-hop/rap recording, the control room may be like the studio control room along with a smaller sized studio to handle the vocals and other instrumentalists.

The misnamed studio

A digital audio production studio (where I live every day of my working life, 8-14 hours a day) is often misnamed as a home studio or project studio. That's because all studios are project studios, and many are in homes, at least in Los Angeles.

Since summer 2000, drastic changes in technology have made the single PC or Mac, a formidable studio in the hands of the capable. And when that's expanded to a two-computer system with GigaStudio on the second system, anyone, anywhere in the world with the right sample libraries, requisite music, and mixing skills, can do high caliber musical productions to the extent that samples can take you.

When expanded to a third computer using a little known PC program called Samplitude 2496, complete post production, CD mastering and film scoring can be done.

With all three computers and a reasonable mixing board, less than 100 square feet is needed. In fact, an extremely powerful two-computer system production studio can operate in under 36 square feet.

Typical digital audio production studio

Below is a simple studio made up of a sequencing/digital audio computer, GigaStudio, one master keyboard controller, the various audio cards and MIDI interfaces, and a Mackie 32-8 bus mixing board.

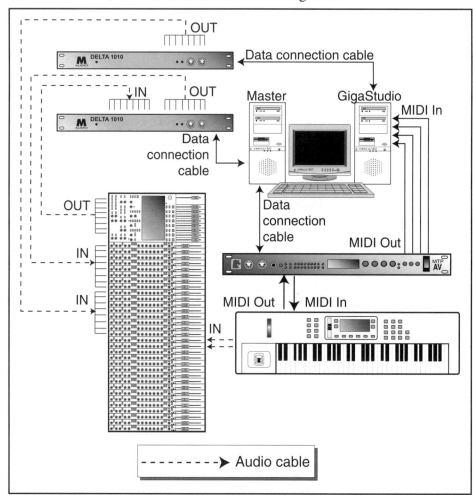

The system is expanded by adding selected MIDI modules, virtual instruments within the host program, and expanding the libraries within GigaStudio. When video syncing is required, either a MOTU Digital Time Piece is added, or the Aardsync II so the whole system can lock to SMPTE time code for film/video scoring purposes. In my studio, I mostly use GigaStudio, but I have older samplers in the Roland and Emu formats that enable me to read what we call "native" CDs vs. using samples translated from one format to another. I also have a few specialty units for unique sounds and ambiances.

Change agents: softsynths and softsamplers

It's the development of the softsynth and softsampler that's fueled a major technological revolution since summer 2000. That's when GigaStudio by NemeSys Technology of Austin, Texas was released.

With GigaStudio 160 in a single computer, we composers finally had for perhaps $3500 (including software, hardware and monitor) a system that was better than the equal of four comparable hardware samplers totalling $20,000. Even with a street discount of 20%, $3500 vs. $16,000 represented (then and now) a considerable saving. But GigaStudio goes beyond that. The maximum capacity of most hardware samplers is 128MB, 256MB at best. With the PC, the limit is the size of your hard drive. And today, a 60GB Maxtor drive can be had for about $150 dollars. You can't compare 128MB to 60GB! And as of summer 2001, all the major hardware sample libraries used in Los Angeles production work, have converted to GigaStudio.

Consider the chart below. For a major work here, at minimum, are the samples needed for each section of the electronic string orchestra using the Kirk Hunter strings (www.ilio.com).

Violins	Violas
Vlns hard with expression	Vlas hard with expression
Vlns hard	Vlas hard
Vlns expressive only	Vlas expressive only
Vlns marcato	Vlas marcato
Vlns pizzicato	Vlas pizzicato
Vlns tremolo	Vlas tremolo
Vlns trill up (1/2 step)	Vlas trill up (1/2 step)
Vlns trill up (whole step)	Vlas trill up (whole step)
Cellos	**Basses**
Cellos hard with expression	Basses hard
Cellos hard	Basses expressive
Cellos expressive only	Basses expressive only
Cellos marcato	Basses marcato
Cellos pizzicato	Basses pizzicato
Cellos tremolo	Basses tremolo
Cellos trill up (1/2 step)	Basses trill up (1/2 step)
Cellos trill up (whole step)	Basses trill up (whole step)

To load all these samples would require just under 300MB of RAM. That's three hardware units just for memory issues. The screen shot of GigaStudio that opened this section shows half the strings loaded in just one screen. Now here's the implementation in Emagic Logic Platinum: With a single click using one external device (GigaStudio), everything needed is available, literally, at the composers right hand. Special effects libraries can also be loaded, enabling the composer or songwriter to not only do the music but drop all kinds of SFX, from car chases to thunderstorms. As a result, production time is greatly sped up, which is crucial in a town where speed to market for TV and film projects is critical.

GigaStudio is the top example today of a software synth. It can reside on its own computer or within the same computer as the sequencing program (for an in depth review of GigaStudio, please see How MIDI Works 6th Edition published by Hal Leonard Corporation).

Virtual instruments

Cubase and Emagic have VST Plug-in folders where these units reside. Cakewalk Sonar has followed the Windows direction with the new DXi plug-in standard. These software programs are complete synthesizers that live in your computer. So rather than expand by buying new MIDI keyboards (at $1600 and up), you expand by getting a new softsynth.

The B4 by Native Instruments

This is a virtual synth version of a Hammond B3 that, with correct set up within the computer, lets you play both manuals and the foot pedals.

The PPG Wave

Here's the PPG Wave "analog" keyboard. All the dials work by being turned by the mouse.

The LM4

Created by my colleagues at Wizoo in Germany, here's a complete drum machine called the LM 4. The sounds come from sampled drum sets residing in the computer's audio drive.

The power of one

Think about it. If you have one good computer, a great MIDI keyboard, and various softsynths, what else do you need? Not much. Both Cubase and Emagic have their own softsamplers (Halion and the EXS24 respectively). To take maximum advantage, you need a powerful system, a lot of RAM, and an audio card with lots of outs.

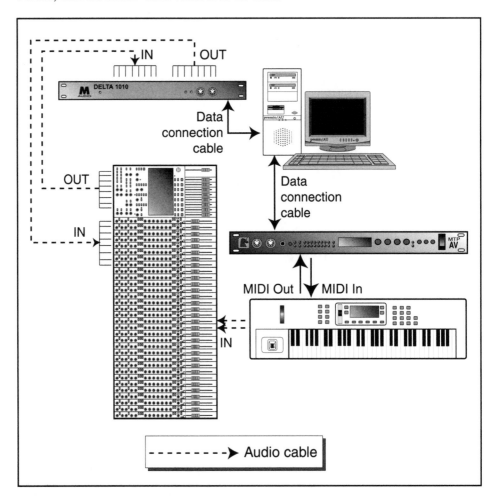

Beyond the core studio

Once the core studio is set, you begin specialization. So, if you want to do film scoring, you add certain syncing devices, a TV monitor, cassette deck, and so on. If you're going to add vocals or instrumentals, you add mics and mic stands.

The "Ikea console"
your advanced digital production studio

The advanced studio comes by adding, interestingly enough, a second monitor! The first monitor is for the sequencing, while the second is for the audio recording. With either the Mac or the PC, you can create a two monitor system by changing your video card, to what's called a dual head card. Matrox is the preferred card and the one most recommended by software manufacturers.

The table is from IKEA ($179 US). Underneath the first monitor (see below) is where the QWERTY keyboard goes. A small rack unit can fit under the table, or get a larger one and set it next to the table. In the rack, we have a MOTU MIDI Time Piece, Delta 1010, and several sound modules.

Mixing Board

Either a mixing board or small rack mount mixer is needed to round out the studio. For the mixing board, you could use a large Mackie or a digital board. You'll learn about these boards later. If this is a MIDI-based digital audio production studio, then a master keyboard would be added.

The three monitor system

This set up is growing in Los Angeles. The left computer system with two monitors can either be a Mac or PC. The second system, with GigaStudio, is a PC system that has two monitors for the sequencing and audio recording and the third for GigaStudio. The remaining equipment options are as described previously.

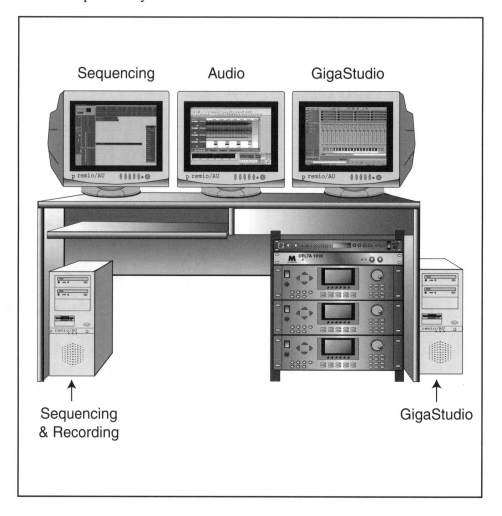

The second three monitor system

This is a three-monitor three-computer system. If you're recording into Samplitude, get a KVM box and let GigaStudio and Samplitude share the same monitor. If you're using a Pro Tools system, you can find a monitor that will work with both the Mac and PC.

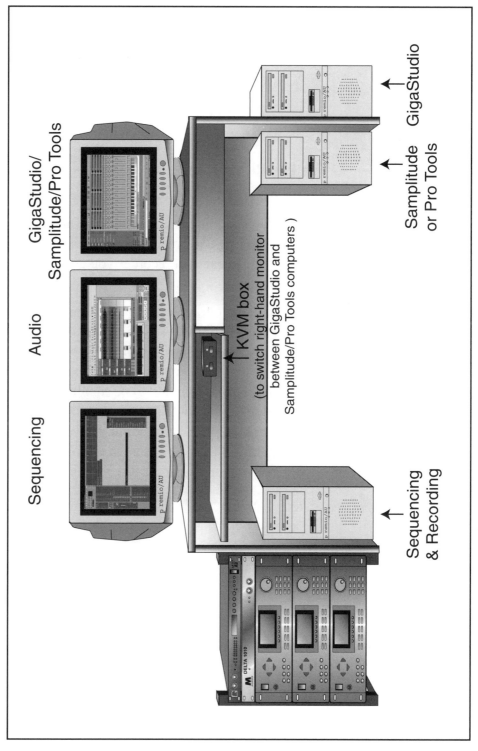

Home recording in the advanced digital production studio

These set ups can be the basis of a small project studio, a post production studio, or a full fledged film/tv scoring studio.

OK, let's suppose you want to record something other than synths or samplers. Well, you now have the same issue as everyone else doing home recording, you have to:

1. Find the right spots in your home to record

2. Work out the cabling and mic stands from wherever your computer is to wherever you want to record.

3. Practice.

The key differences

1. You're recording directly into the computer.

2. You're adding effects, generally after you've done the recording and are applying the effects to the audio file. With an external recorder you generally add outside effects boxes.

3. You can't drag the computer everywhere you want to go! Like a traditional studio, you're operating in a fixed place. This may seem overly obvious, but it's the obvious things that people often miss in their excitement to learn recording. So you're going to be running cable from the mixing board to whatever room you're trying to record in. If you're just going to be bringing in the occasional musician, then ultimately look to set up in a room large enough to record both another person and your regular projects.

Home Recording With a 4-Track

Having reviewed both a major studio and a digital audio production studio, we now want to look more closely at a series of project studios you're most like to create in your home. We start with a 4-track cassette deck. Working with a 4-track cassette deck can at first appear to be very limiting when compared to working with "junior" digital audio production programs like Cakewalk Home Studio, Cubasis (from Steinberg) or Micrologic (from Emagic), all of which retail for under $100 US. That's because even the junior programs have:

1. a virtual mixing board

2. effects

3. ability to record up to 16 digital audio tracks (Micrologic AV)

4. Rocket Network enabled for online distance education classes

However, while you do have these "goodies" within the software programs, there is still very good reason to start your recording experience with tape. With these thoughts in mind, turn the page and look at our drawing of the Tascam 424 mkIII Portastudio which uses high bias cassette tape to record on.

The Tascam 424 mkIII Portastudio

To make learning simpler, we'll look from left to right.

The Tascam mkIII is a combination console/recorder. It contains the mixing board and the recorder. Below you see a series of sliders. These are called *faders*, because they fade the volume levels up or down.

The channel strip

Above the faders are the mute, solo and pan knobs. Mute silences one or more tracks out of the six, while leaving the remaining tracks to play. Solo works the opposite. It lets you pull out one or more tracks while silencing the rest. The pan knob positions the sound in the stereo spectrum from left to right. Above the pan knob are the positions for Effects 1 and 2. In a traditional analog board, these effects positions will be above the next section, called the EQ section. There are several different types of EQ. This one is called a three-band parametric EQ.

Above the EQ are the mic/line switches. When switched to mic (pronounced *mike*), the console is set to handle a microphone input. When set to line, it's set to handle a guitar, bass, or MIDI keyboard. In short, any instrument with a line input.

Above the mic/line switch is a knob that's called trim or gain, depending on the manufacturer. Regardless of the name, its purpose is to help set the amount of volume level coming into the board.

All of the elements we've just looked at and identified make up the *channel strip*. The excellent thing about the Tascam 424 mkIII is that the channel strip is the junior version of a much larger sized board. Once you've learned how to work the channel strip on any board, you can pretty much run this board.

The master

The seventh slider is the Master volume fader and it controls the total volume.

The meter bridge

Above the transport buttons to the far right is a junior meter bridge. Meters visualize the volume levels and aid you in adjusting the faders, gain/trim.

The transport

This is where you control stop, play, record, fast forward, fast reverse (also called cueing).

The remaining buttons have to do with features specific to the 424.

Key learning advantage

The key advantage of this Portastudio is that it's most like a full-sized mixing board. What you learn here is immediately transferrable to a larger board. Also, the focus of this unit is on recording, not button pushing routines. So while it will be more costly to build the studio because of having to acquire outside effects, your actual learning curve is shorter because you're skipping the intermediate technological step of having to learn the button pushing routines and the *concept* of recording before you ever get to *learn* how to record. With this unit, you just start recording.

By comparison, learning the virtual mixing boards within a software program (any of them) or working with a digital recorder can be daunting if you have no previous experience recording. That's because both software and digital units often work with non-standard layouts, and methods of working that are not intuitive, often even to professionals.

The downside

The two biggest downsides compared to digital units and software is that your music is stored on a small tape vs. a hard drive for immediate recall, and it doesn't come with an internal effects package. However, judicious shopping on Ebay can easily remedy the latter critique. Also, because you are using tape, you're not going to get the same sound as working with a top notch high end digital recorder or software program. But if you're just starting out and you're just looking to practice recording your songs and build technique, then go for it. It's a great piece and you'll learn a lot.

Next up

Next is the Roland BR-8 Digital Recorder.

4
Home Recording With the Roland BR-8 Digital Recorder

With the Roland BR-8 Digital Recorder, we enter the Space Age. In one small unit that can fit into a typical briefcase, you have a console/recorder/*studio*. All three. Inside the BR-8 is an 8-track digital recorder, console, effects, and the ability to save your work to a Zip disk. You can do multiple tracks and takes. Included is a sketch pad feature (great for guitarists) that lets you develop your original songs and hear them back. Because storage is data storage on a Zip disk, instead of being limited by the time on a tape, your restrictions are the capacity of the Zip disk, which happens to be 100MB.

For many, the BR-8 is their very first recorder. So not only must recording be learned, but so must the concepts behind analog recording that have been grafted into the digital technology.

Before you turn the page, keep in mind what I taught you in the last chapter. The Tascam unit is most like a "real" mixing board. Once you understand that board, your knowledge can be immediately transferred to most any other recorder. Thanks to miniaturization, with the BR-8, you're getting an incredibly value priced package. But also thanks to miniaturization, you're working with a non-standard design. So certain concepts easy to see on a Tascam or a Mackie board, are not as easy to visualize with this tiny titan. This is not a criticism, simply a training observation. Having said that, turn the page.

Where's the channel strip?

In the last chapter, I spent time explaining the channel strip on the Tascam 424 MKIII. To the left is the channel strip of the Mackie 32-8 bus board. If you take a few minutes to read the labeling on the channel strip, you'll notice a lot of similarities to what you saw on the Tascam (compare below in the lower right hand corner of this page). Because they're similar in concept and design, you can quickly transfer the knowledge gained from the Tascam Portastudio to the larger Mackie board. Remember this principle, *once you've learned the channel strip you've mostly learned the board.*

Now look at the BR-8 on the next page. Ask this question: Where's the channel strip? If your answer is, "I don't know," you're right! And neither do I.

That's because the smaller digital units, capitalizing on miniaturized circuits, implement the channel strip as a *concept*, but *not* as a visual design like a traditional mixing board.

This means that the first task in learning *any* digital recorder is to start with finding the channel strip (fader, pan, mute, solo, EQ, gain/trim, aux sends, mic/line inputs). Once you've found them, you're halfway home. But this brings up another issue that the technologists and their board designs have overlooked.

Look below. See how all the EQ volume levels and effects are cleanly and clearly laid out for you on the Tascam 424? This means that when you go to do the final mix, everything is in front of you. You can see all the knobs and faders. On a hardware digital recorder, this is not always the case. Nor is it on some virtual mixing boards. This means that the mixing process can become more cumbersome and confusing, not only because of poor layouts, but also because of information overload.

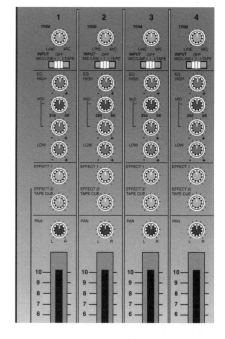

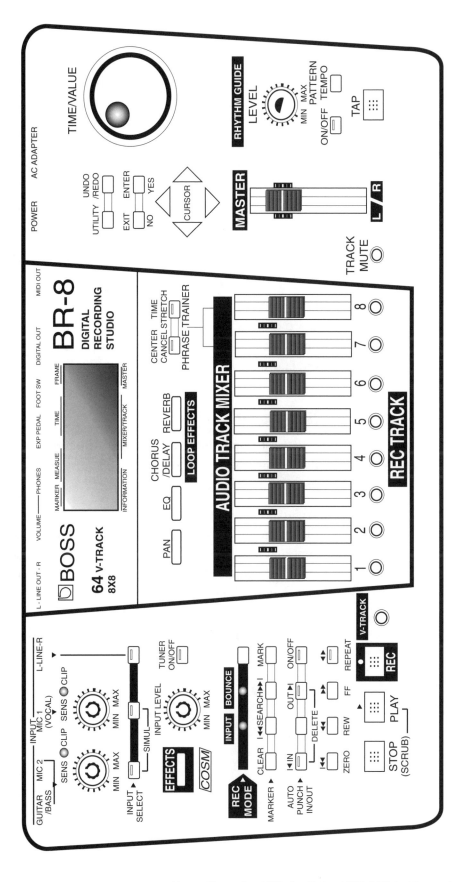

Automating the mix - a software advantage

An advantage found on larger more expensive boards is the ability to automate the mix, then save it for future use. To do that on a hardware board, the faders have to either be motorized, or you need a separate mini-computer that connects to the board to remember all your moves. You can do this automatically on all the major virtual mixing boards. To make a change on any board (Mackie to Tascam to....) during the mix, requires manual moves to do so.

This is one reason why EQ'ing is left for the final mix, often after the effects have been applied. It's another reason why big hardware boards with lots of channel strips are very popular.

In general, the more channel strips you have on your mixing board, the greater control you have in the mix.

For example, if the snare drum is on its own channel strip, you can EQ the snare drum alone as it sounds within the total mix. If you have the entire drum set on the channel strip, you can't focus. Instead, you can *only* EQ the entire set as it sounds within the mix.

Summary

The most important lesson of these first group of lessons is to understand the engineer's rule of thumb: *If you can run one channel strip, you largely know how to run the mixing board.*

We've now seen an analog unit and a small digital unit. The analog unit has the mixing board portion clearly laid out, looking very similar in both concept and design to the larger hardware mixing board. By comparison, the smaller feature rich digital units operate by the concept of the channel strip board, without incorporating the traditional layout. So if you've had no previous experience with recording, grasping some of the concepts and signal flow can be more difficult, and as such, extend the learning curve a bit.

Next up

We'll look at the larger Roland VS1880 unit and see how these concepts apply.

5 Recording With the Roland VS1880

Once upon a time there was a harp player in New York City. She spent $10,000 US at a New York recording studio to produce her first harp album. Not knowing anything about recording or how to pick an engineer (to determine his experience recording solo harp or other orchestral instruments), she trusted him to do a good job. The result: a horrendous recording. Determined that this not happen again, she went and bought, as her first recorder, the Roland VS1680 and the two effects boards you can buy that give 1000 effects (a thousand effects!!!). When she got it home, she sat on the floor and opened up the box. Looking at the 1680, she broke down and began to cry. She couldn't find the On button.

Now, this true story is indicative of the kinds of reasons folks are buying the larger Roland VS recorders. They want to record and produce their own CD (perfectly valid) without getting screwed because they have no experience recording (another perfectly valid consideration). And the Roland VS units are an excellent unit. They've got everything (and I mean everything, including CD mastering and burning). So while expensive, they are also *incredibly* value priced because of what you get and what you can do.

But, if you've had no previous experience doing recording of some kind, the 1680, 1880 and now 2480 series can be incredibly daunting.

To avoid that problem, we'll start "undaunting" the 1880 as soon as you turn the page.

Where's the channel strip?

OK, Mackie strip to the left, Roland VS1880 to the right. Asking the question, "Where's the channel strip?" yields the same answer: "I don't know."

This is going to be the answer with nearly all hardware digital recorders and some software recorders.

Again, once you've located the parts of the channel strip, you're on your way to recording more quickly and understanding how the unit works.

With that, you must log down the button pushing steps (and screens) you go through to get to each piece of the channel strip. So for the VS unit, as an example, above the faders are the track buttons with labeling for pan, EQ, etc.

You also see the inputs at the top of the unit. So now, you search for the rest of the mixing board.

Now, the VS is also a recorder. So for me, the next procedural steps would be how to work the recorder portion.

Notice my priority: *first* the board, *then* the recorder. Most want to start with the recorder. And you can certainly do that, but in the long run, the shorter learning curve is to be patient, learn the mixing board first (called signal flow) then progress to the recorder potions.

Now where's the channel strip?

To the left is the Mackie channel strip, to the right is the C-Console for the VS1680 as created by C-MEXX. When the question, "Where's the channel strip?" is asked, we get a visual answer with this program. The C-MEXX Console works with the VS1880 via MIDI control through your PC. The first thing you'll notice is that the graphical user interface (GUI) is laid out like a standard mixing board. Using C-MEXX can help put the VS1680 or 1880 onto more familiar ground. As long as you have a MIDI card in your computer, you just connect a MIDI cable from the computer to the MIDI jack on the back of either the VS1680 or VS1880. The mouse moves the faders on the C-MEXX console. In turn, you can watch the faders move on the VS units.

Thus, by learning both the recorder and the C-MEXX software, you can automate the mix for your songs, and quickly get at the marvelous features built into the VS series units.

Key Lesson

Recording/mixing is as visual as it is aural.

Summary

Like it's kid brother the BR-8, the mixing board portion of the VS1880 is laid out by concept, but not by the traditional design and layout of a mixing board. Not only does it have the mixing board built in, but also the digital recorder. Like the BR-8, once you've located the channel strip features, you're halfway home to operations.

In a professional studio, the mixing board and recorder are two totally separate pieces as are the effects. With the BR-8, VS1880, and Korg D-Series units, the mixing board, the recorder and the effects are fixed in one place, thus giving you complete and total portability.

Thus, the control room and the studio are in the same room as the VS unit. There's no separation as in a larger studio.

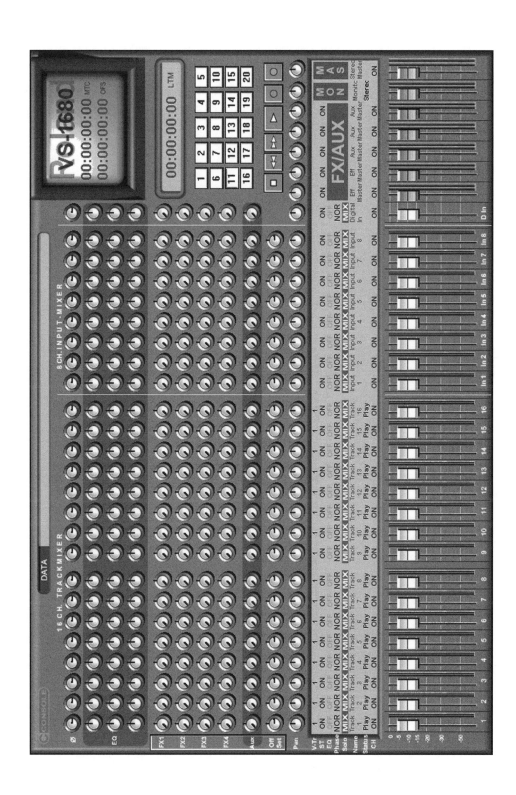

What's next?

We've looked at hardware studio considerations. Now we're going to look at the set ups within, Cubase, Emagic and Samplitude 2496.

Recording With Software Recorders

So far we've looked at hardware units to set your expectations for recording at home. We've learned that both the recorder and the mixing board are contained in the single unit. Thus, the room you record in is both control room and studio. We've learned that if you can operate the channel strip, you can largely operate the board. In an analog unit like the Tascam or larger Mackie board, concept and design merge to create an operational procedure that's transferrable from one board to another. With a digital unit, because of miniaturized circuits, you have to find the channel strip, because those boards are laid out by the concept of how a mixing board works, and don't have a consistent design from one system to another. As a result, knowledge is not as easily transferred should you find yourself needing to work with a more "traditional" board.

A major feature shift

Except for the rare system, PC DAWs (music computers) are not portable like the VS or Portastudio class units. They come with an audio card that connects to a mixing board. Thus, your recording and mixing are done in the same room unless you so design your studio so that the PC resides in a control room (where it doubles as a recorder), and you look into a room used as the recording studio. Carefully study the diagram on the next page so that this concept is clear to you.

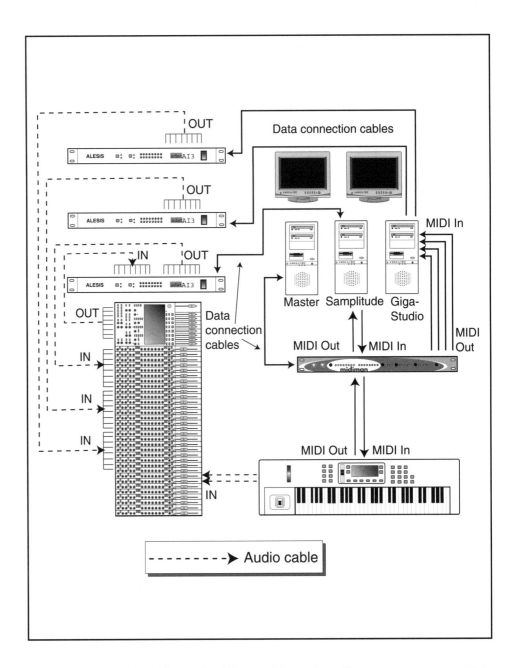

Take a good look at this studio. It's too big to drag from room to room! It's fixed and decidedly non-portable. Before you start spending money, you need to be very clear what your recording objectives are, the equipment you need, and where you're going to record.

Disappearance of the dividing line
between pro and consumer recording software

A few years ago there was a clear difference between professional and consumer grade sequencing and digital audio recording programs. With the exception of a handful of programs, that line is gone. Today, albums, movies and TV shows are created using Cakewalk, Cubase, Emagic Logic, Performer (a Mac-only program) and Samplitude 2496. The street price of most of these programs is about $600.

The teaching point is that *all* the software mentioned is *professional* software. So you can have in your home or school the same stuff the pro's use, as long as you understand that it's knowing *how* to use it that determines whether or not you get professional sounding results. Today, with this software and the appropriate computer set up, you can do for around $3500 - $4500 (including small mixing board) what some professionals spend $20,000, $30,000, even $50,000 to achieve within a computer-based system.

So as we look at these programs, you need to be mindful that you can get incredible results provided you put in the time and set your computer up correctly.

Working with a software recording program

There are four basic types of software recording programs.

- a full package consisting of sequencer, notation, digital audio, audio editing

- recording only with little or no MIDI implementation, but strong emphasis on recording, post-production and multimedia features.

- mastering programs that can record in stereo but whose main purpose is to take the final audio files and prepare them for CD mastering.

- audio editing for recording and sound design

Full packages

These are Cubase, Emagic Logic, Performer/Digital Performer on the Mac, and Sonar. Each of these has sequencing, notation, digital audio and audio editing. They also allow for expanding the system by way of virtual instruments and effects plug-ins.

Junior full packages

Each of the major companies has a junior full package retailing for under $100 US. While there is a shorter learning curve for operations, the curve for learning recording is still the same. Regardless of the program's price, whatcha gotta know is whatcha gotta know.

Recording only

These include Cool Edit Pro, Digi 001, Nuendo, Pro Tools, Samplitude 2496, Sequoia, and Vegas Audio. Software pricing on these programs runs from $399 up to $20,000 or more. Cool Edit Pro clocks in at $399, Digi 001 at around $1500 for the whole package, Nuendo starts at $1200, Pro Tools can run from $10,000 and up depending on how your system is configured. It's not uncommon to find $20,000 and $40,000 Pro Tools systems. Samplitude, the more unknown of the group, is only $719 and is both a multitrack recorder with MIDI implementation, and a mastering program capable of burning a Red Book standard CD within the program. It has excellent video implementation, and so, permits both film and multimedia production projects to be done on it. Sequoia is Samplitude's big brother and lists at just under $3800, although you can buy it off the SEK'D website for just under $2800. Except for a few features really needed by professionals used to working with systems by Sonic Solutions and Dyaxis, Samplitude and Sequoia are largely the same program.

Mastering software programs

A mastering program is one in which your final audio files are prepared for recording (mastering) to CD. These programs record in stereo only, although you can direct record in them. For the PC, Sound Forge continues to dominate as an absolutely top drawer program. Wavelab from Steinberg is also enjoying an excellent reputation. Not as well known is Samplitude Master, the two-track mastering version of Samplitude 2496. There are certainly other programs, but these are both the best well known and the ones most used in professional work.

Audio editing programs

These are programs used to edit audio files and for sound design in motion picture and TV work. There are three programs best known for this kind of work: Cool Edit Pro, Sound Forge, and Samplitude. At the higher end, you can also do sound design in Pro Tools.

Which to pick?

You need two. One to do the sequencing and recording in, and the other to do mastering and burn the CD to Red Book standard. Study the chart below.

	Seq/DAR	Rec Only/ little MIDI	Mastering	Burn CD	Snd Design
Cakewalk	X				
Cool Edit Pro		X			X
Cubase	X				
Emagic Logic	X				
Performer	X				
Samplitude		X	X	X	X
Sound Forge			X	X	X
Vegas Audio		X			
Wavelab			X	X	X

For sequencing/digital audio recording

If notation is important to you, look at Cubase and Emagic Logic, and to some degree to Performer.

If notation is unimportant to you, look at Cakewalk Sonar.

For multitrack recording only

Look at Cool Edit Pro, Samplitude and Vegas.

For mastering

Look at Sound Forge, Samplitude and Wave Lab.

Why two programs

A software program is a tool. So the idea is to pick the right tool for the job. Another consideration is how much time you have to learn programs vs. getting the work done.

If you're doing sequencing and recording, then you'll pick two programs. One for the sequencing/digital audio recording, and the other for mastering and CD burning to Red Book standard. As a working professional, I want to restrict my choices to working with a program that has enough features to save me from learning several programs. So for our purposes, we mostly use Emagic and Cubase with Samplitude. We chose this combination because of the notation features which are strong enough for the book and music publishing we do. It also saves us from having to learn a full fledged graphic driven notation program like Finale or Sibelius. Both programs are patrons of the Rocket Network, and so let us run "live" online classes and labs.

There are certain projects we do in Cakewalk Sonar because of the multimedia applications for the Web.

The point is clear: each program has a strength or a set of strengths. Because we can define the kind of work we're doing, we're able to assess these programs in light of our documented needs and production goals.

Full package vs. recording only

When should you use a full program vs. a recording only program? The easiest answer is that if you're not looking to do MIDI recording with a sequencer, then you should consider going direct to the recording only programs.

Or, if you're doing serious multimedia/film/tv work, then you should consider opting for a separate dedicated computer whose purpose is recording only.

There are several pragmatic reasons for my opinion.

1. The overall trend of the sequencing/recording programs is to be an all-in-one turnkey setup with softsynths, notation, sequencing and digital audio recording. Thus, the learning curve is quite steep.

2. The overall trend of the recording only programs is for, well, recording! Along with video implementation for multimedia and film/tv scoring. Thus, you're working with a focused program with a focused goal - recording.

3. The more a program does, regardless of the platform, somewhere it will hit a peak. Having a second dedicated computer for just digital recording is a career failsafe. If something happens, your career isn't shut down.

This opinion comes from watching "full strength" programs shut down with an audio driver or update change. The focused audio recording programs are not subject to the winds of audio driver change. Samplitude and Vegas operate with Windows MME. Nuendo operates with ASIO 2 and works best with the RME Hammerfall Digi9652 card. Cool Edit Pro operates with MME. The point: *stability*.

This approach can also eliminate certain syncing issues that come up with these programs. For example, it's very common in professional circles to sequence in Cubase or Emagic and record into Pro Tools. On the PC, you can do the same thing by recording into Samplitude. Here's a potential system set up that could be labeled, "the works."

The Works!

This is a powerful studio set up giving you the option of recording in either the master computer (Cubase, Emagic, Sonar) and the recording computer, here Samplitude, but it could equally be Cool Edit Pro, Nuendo, Pro Tools or one of several other programs. I showed it earlier in the chapter, but to reinforce our key learning points, here it is repeated.

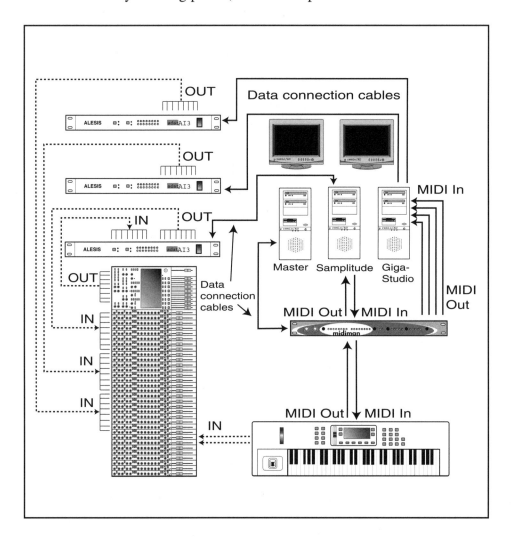

Warning! Multiple learning curves

When you get into a computer-based program, you have a learning curve that's literally exponential vs. arithmetic. With the portable units, you're basically learning operations and how to record. With a computer, Mac or PC, you must learn about the OS (operating system), each major part of the software program, have an audio card and MIDI interface, have a mixing board and learn how to run the board, etc., etc., etc!

What you need depends on what you want to accomplish. I couldn't do my career on a portable unit. I've got to have the larger computer system. But if I just wanted to do song demos, maybe develop a basic album for myself, then I'm going for the Korg, Roland or Tascam units because that's all you need. If your goal is composing, film scoring, sound design, hip hop, Rap, R&B, etc., then you're looking at a computer-based system because of the incredible production tools available to you (like Acid, Fruity Loops, Reason, Reaktor, etc.)

Deep learning curves

Remember what I said earlier in the chapter. These are professional programs that let you do nearly anything you want. The notion of instant gratification and creating sumptuous sounding productions 12 minutes after you've got it out of the box is a lie. It's that simple. When you have a professional program that combines smaller programs into the larger whole, you have to learn how to work each one of them. You can't escape it. It's not avoidable.

And if you're doing this for fun, and you're not patient, and you like to use the word "should" a lot, find another hobby because you won't be happy unless you happen to be into self-punishment.

On the other hand, if you're willing to accept the learning curve and set your computer up correctly, you've got a wonderful world of expressive, powerful software that will empower you to record and publish your music on CD, MP3, Windows Media, Real Audio, or even in print. This is the best time in the whole world to learn recording. I confess, it was a hill. But I've largely climbed over it and I'm thankful to God everyday for it, because it lets me do what I otherwise could only dream about doing.

Next...

Having set your expectations, we'll now look at Cubase 5.0.

Recording With Cubase 32 5.0

7

With this and the next chapter, we'll look at recording with two full programs, Cubase and Emagic. These programs contain a sequencer, a virtual MIDI mixing board, a notation package for score printing, a digital audio recorder, a digital audio virtual mixer, audio editing and effects, and the ability to do either stereo or surround mixing. All in one package.

Differences between a software recorder and hardware recorder

To review again, with the Tascam and Roland units, we've seen the console and recorder built into a single unit. While you get a virtual mixing board within the software program, reality is that you need a separate mixing board, because the audio card with its multiple audio outs and ins requires it. If you're just learning at home, and your PC has a Soundblaster card, you can avoid the mixing board for a bit by using your computer speaker system. But ultimately, to do professional work, you need an audio card with multiple outs especially if you're using GigaStudio, GigaSampler, or other virtual instruments within the host sequencing program.

Cubase and Emagic come with a range of 20 to 50 effects plug-ins within the program. Hardware units require that you either buy external hardware effects units or, as in the case of the Roland VS units, effects cards. VS units at this writing are designed for a maximum of two effects boards. Each board contains 500 effects. So with two boards, you're working your way through 1000 effects presets!

How professionals record

In Los Angeles, for film/TV work, the most common approach is to use a two-three computer system. In the master computer, the sequence is built and then recorded into a second computer, 99.9% of the time using Pro Tools as the software recorder. Next, "live" musicians are added to the recording session. Work is often done with the effects being recorded at the same time as all the other musicians and MIDI tracks. This is most often done with high end professional effects units, and high end TDM plug-ins (which work in Pro Tools).

However, depending on budgets, recording can be done directly into Cubase. VST effects plug-ins can be used, but more often high end hardware effects units are used. In this procedure, you're recording through a mixing board with effects added. This lets you hear the whole piece before recording it.

With Cubase and the ASIO 2 audio driver, you can record and monitor sound going in and out the program, and with that, apply the internal VST plug-ins before you record.

The third computer to be added is GigaStudio.

Where's the channel strip?

To the left is our Mackie channel strip. Below is the Inspector area in the Cubase arrange window.

This is the first of two Inspectors, one for MIDI and one for digital audio. Look for Pan and Volume. Then look for Solo. Under the column labeled M (mute) you'll see where I muted a track. What you're seeing is a different way of laying out the key parts of a channel fader in a MIDI environment.

Now we've made a change in Cubase. To the left is the Mackie channel strip. Now I've added Volume and Pan to the layout in the Arrange window. Notice that horizontal faders appear to control panning and volume. This means that for each audio or MIDI track, I can mix right on the main screen!

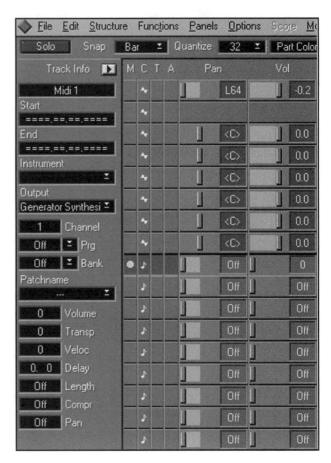

Now I've clicked on an audio track. Notice how the Inspector changes. Also, with audio files, I can do a basic mix right in the Arrange window. Again, compare to the Mackie strip to the left. Look carefully in the Inspector area and you'll see INS DYN and FX EQ.

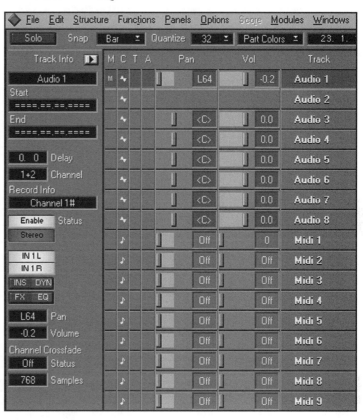

Now where's the channel strip?

I've clicked the FX/EQ button and now appears for that stereo pair, the Cubase virtual channel strip. Comparing this to the Mackie, you find the channel fader, mute, solo and pan where you'd normally expect it. Reading to the right are Inserts (4) followed by Aux Sends (8) then the EQ. This design is actually the reverse order of a typical mixing board. Inserts are normally at the very top of a board, then the Aux Sends, then EQ, then the channel fader.

Differences between the hardware and virtual board

With the hardware board (whether the Tascam or the Mackie), all your changes are made by knobs and they're all in front of you. This is a design issue, but it's also a work flow issue. The eyes and hands move by order of greatest order and priority.

The Cubase virtual board is a graphic approach to mixing. So when you make EQ changes (Cubase features a 4-band parametric EQ) you have to open and close each of the strips you're working on.

Now, on this shot is the VST mixing board. Notice that the layout shows the channel faders only plus mute, solo, and pan. To get to EQ, you click on FX/EQ. So this means that if you have to EQ seven or eight channel faders, you have to open seven or eight individual screens to do it.

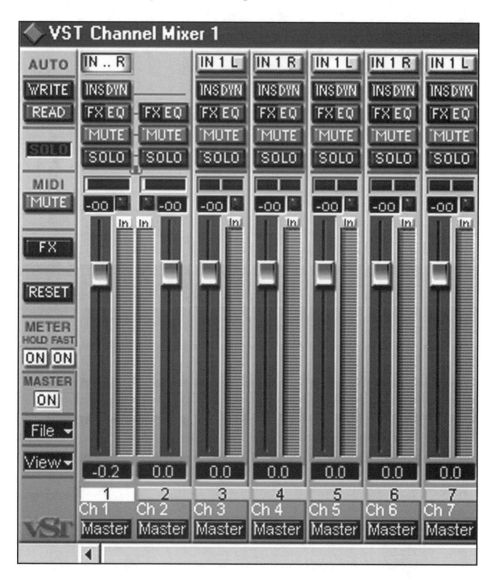

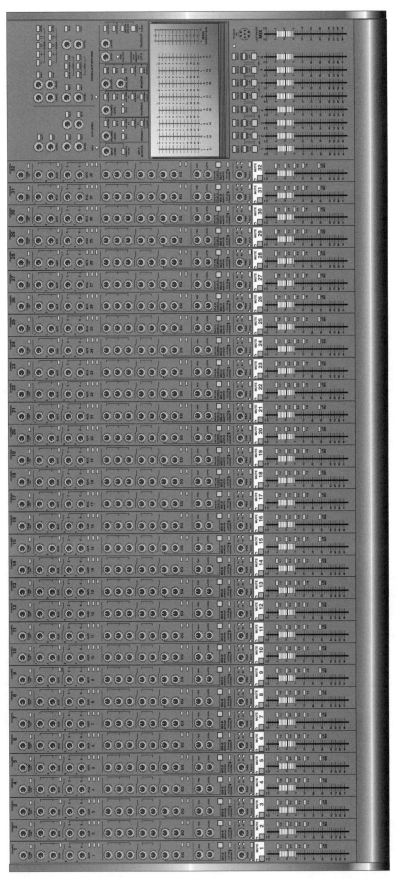

Now, for the final comparison, look at the Mackie 32-8 bus analog board and notice the layout compared to the internal VST board on the opposite page.

Which does a professional use?

Depends on the situation. When we're in a hurry, we set the mix up at the Mackie board with the effects we want to use and record the final result either within the audio program, or to DAT, or to ADAT, or to Tascam DA88, or to Pro Tools, or to Samplitude 2496. The correct answer is, it depends.

Next

We'll do a similar comparison with Logic.

Recording With Emagic Logic Platinum

Like Cubase, Emagic is also a full strength program. It has a sequencer, a virtual MIDI mixing board, a notation package for score printing, a digital audio recorder, a digital audio virtual mixer, audio editing and effects, and the ability to do either stereo or surround mixing. All in one package.

While Logic is as equally used as Cubase in dance music production, concert work and film/TV production, its general direction is more high end, largely due to its relationship with Pro Tools and integration of TDM plug-ins for the Mac version. With the demise of Opcode and its Vision and Studio Vision recording programs, Emagic has taken a large share of that Mac segment as former users looked for a new program.

Not complex

Over the years, Logic has developed a reputation for being a difficult program to learn. This has been fostered, unfortunately, by the company itself who, looking for what we in marketing call the USP (Unique Selling Proposition) would say to prospective users, "Imagine being inside the computer and making it do whatever you want!" And for a while, they talked about how three-dimensional Logic was compared to other programs. Another sales point was, "not telling you how to sequence, but letting you choose your work method for yourself." Then came, that learning to use Logic was like building a house.

Well, these are all great USPs *if* you wished you had been born as an electron instead of a human being. However, most of the time the thing we'd like to tell our computers to do is, "STOP CRASHING!" And sequencing three-dimensionally? Most people have a hard enough time in two! But three!?

When Emagic went from Notator to Logic, Hank Mancini was still alive and I was his computer tech. Hank used Notator on the Atari, and really loved it. But when Logic came out, we didn't have time to build a house, dictate to a computer, or operate in a three-dimensional sphere.

There are two aspects to working in Hollywood in music that most people don't get. First, it's all politics. And second, it's about working fast. People developing story lines and scripts and special effects for theatrical release motion pictures, can get months to a year to do the technology to get a single scene right.

But not composers. We're most like the US Navy Seabees (Construction Battalion) and our industry assigned motto is, "The improbable we can do, the impossible takes a little longer." This means, we have to get things laid out clear, clean and quick for immediate action. So unfortunately, I moved Hank to a different program. And in previous versions of my *How MIDI Works* book, I downplayed the program, because I couldn't get them to start me where I was - in two-dimensional checkers (vs. three-dimensional chess).

But by the time Logic got into version 3, things were changing, and in version 4 they hit their stride. I got version 3.5 just before 4 came out, and the leap was enormous. This first screen shot is of the main screen of 4.7. Notice the clear, elegant look.

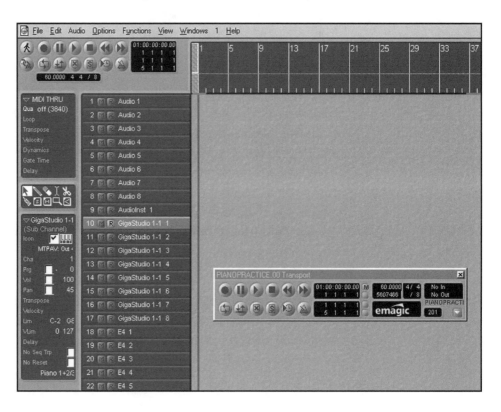

Once Logic 4.0 was loaded and armed with the manual I began working through my recording procedures with Logic. In the end, I found a program that was easy and quick to use, and whose virtual mixing board was modeled after that of a typical analog board, thus allowing me to easily transfer my mixing board knowledge to their board.

In all, with the training we've put together in either our online classes (www.alexuniv.com/AU), or with our Logic 5.0 book, you can be up and running this powerful program productively in just a few hours.

In short, Logic's complexity is largely in the hoopla. This is a feature rich program. And it has a lot of great features. So by its very nature of being feature rich, any program will have a deeper learning curve. But the basic learning curve for learning key work related issues is only a few hours.

Where's the channel strip?

OK, Mackie to the left, Logic below. Notice that the left side of 4.7 has the Volume and Pan (look for the checkmarks). You solo the track with the S on the transport. You mute the track by clicking the M in the Arrange window area.

For individual pan and volume changes, you zoom in and the track expands. You can then make a selection that lets you draw in for the individual sequence, on the main screen your volume edits, pan edits, etc.

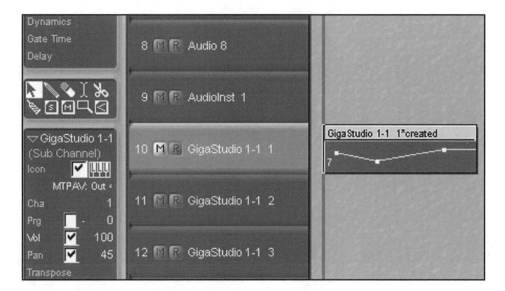

So to compare, with VST, you get onscreen sliders in the Arrange window. With Logic in their Arrange window, you draw in the volume and pan data.

Now where's the channel strip?

Once again, Mackie to the left, the Emagic virtual mixing board below. Here, I've "turned on" the 3-band parametric EQ on five channel strips. So we can immediately look and see the channel fader, mute and solo (at the bottom of the channel fader), the pan knob, the inserts and the sends. Because it's all laid out, I can, like with any traditional mixing board, see the whole mix in front of me.

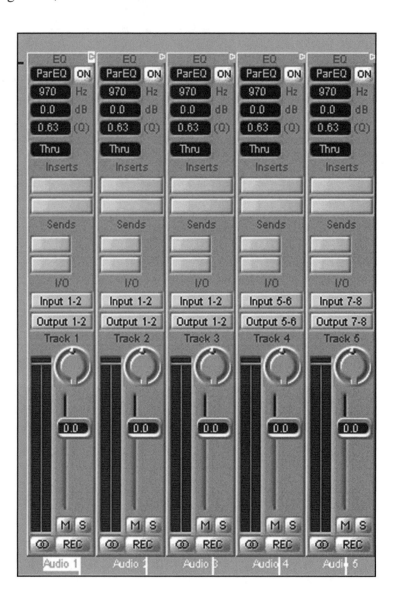

Other EQs

You're not limited with this basic 3-band parametric EQ. With Logic 4.7 comes these individual choices:

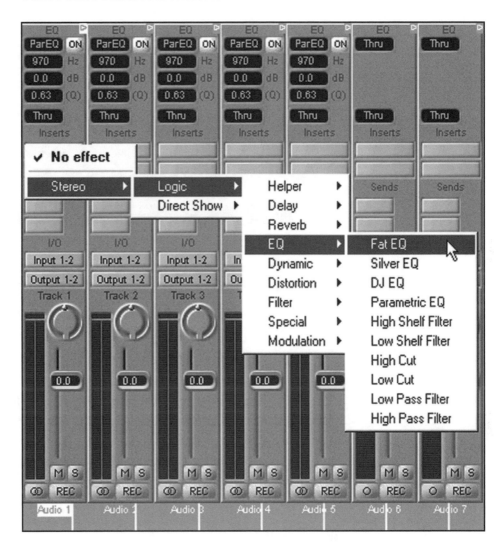

This means that like Cubase, if you select one of these other EQs, you'll have to open the EQ for each channel strip. In fact, this is the case for all the other software recording programs we'll look at. And here's one reason why.

The EQ is treated as an alternative plug-in that can be purchased from another company. This gives you the option of using either the factory EQs or one from another collection. Here, as an example, is the EQ from TC Works Native Essentials, a high end post-production caliber series of plug-ins:

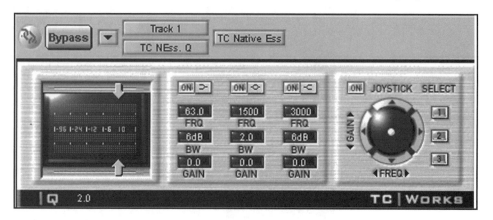

Comparison to a hardware mixing board

With a hardware board, you see everything, and with the EQ, you accept what the board has. With a virtual mixer, you largely give up seeing the EQ on each channel strip, but you gain the choice of selecting which EQ you want.

However! You can also automate your mixes, save them, even create several automated mixes for the same song or work that you can save and reload later. Unless the hardware board has automation built in, or you purchased a separate device for automation, this feature is one of the real benefits of virtual mixing.

What's next

We've looked at two full programs. Now lets look at a dedicated virtual recorder called Samplitude 2496.

Recording With Samplitude 2496

Now, we turn our attention to a dedicated audio recording program, Samplitude 2496. While its name may suggest that it's a sampling program, Samplitude is a software multitrack recorder, advanced audio editor, film scoring program, and mastering program that burns CDs to Red Book standard, the production standard of CD manufacturing.

Samplitude also has MIDI implementation that lets you set up a MIDI click, sequence, set time signature and tempo, and do basic editing. If you need to do a quick sequence, you can do it here. You can also import a MIDI file and have it assigned to its own track. But for advanced sequencing, you'll want to use Cakewalk, Cubase or Emagic.

In my mind, Samplitude 2496 is the "jeep" of digital audio recording because it goes anywhere, does just about anything, and doesn't require proprietary hardware to operate. It also doesn't have specialized audio drivers. Instead, it works with the Windows MME drivers. As a result, any number of excellent audio cards are available for it.

Using an RME Digi 9652 card, you can get 24 ADAT I/Os. But if you use two Digi 9652 cards, you can get 48 ADAT I/Os, all out of a single machine.

For Internet distribution, you can output the final audio to MP3, Windows Media, or Real Audio formats. Starting with version 6.0, you can record direct as an MP3 file.

You can also import video, and separate the audio track from the video. The video then "breaks out" into a storyboard-like frame layout.

You can download a test version at www.magix.com.

Object Editor mixing

Samplitude works on a unique principle you'll soon see imitated in other programs. It's called Object Editor mixing. Below is an audio object within the track that I highlighted. Below that you'll see the button for the Object Editor.

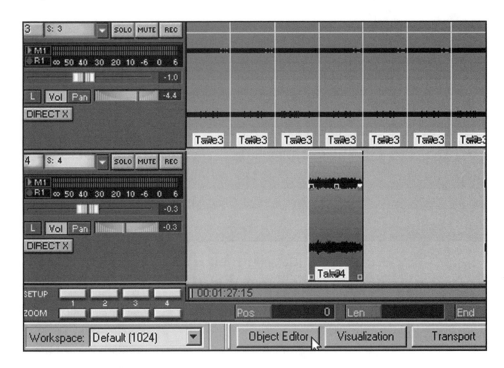

Opening the Object Editor - Effects

Below is one of three windows for the Object Editor. Look in the center of the screen shot and you'll see four bands of EQ. Reading to the right is the compressor. Below that is the Pan for mono or stereo.

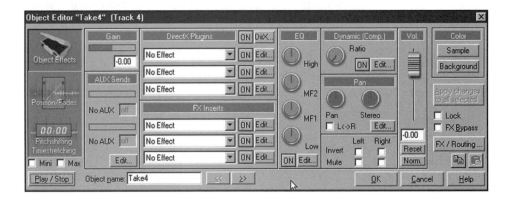

If I click once on Edit, under the Compressor, the Compressor, Expander, Noise Gate and Limiter window opens. Remember, all this for that small object I highlighted.

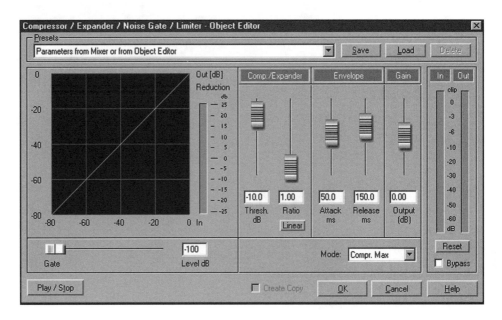

Moving back to center, there's the DirectX button. If I click once on it, the following screen comes up showing me all the DirectX effects I've installed.

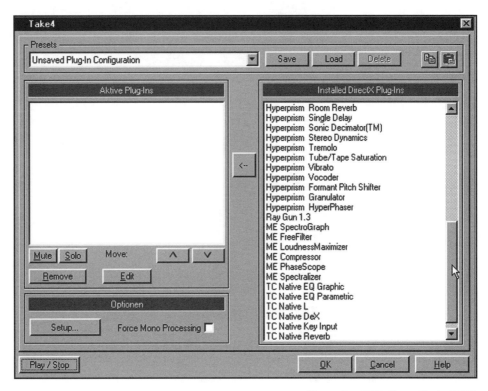

To load the DirectX effect, you just double click. It loads, and then you select the effect you want. Below is the TC Works Native Bundle Reverb.

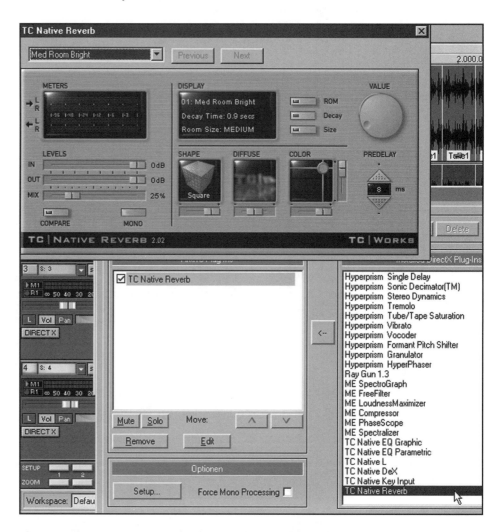

Going back to center, I have below the DirectX effects, FX Inserts. These are native to Samplitude. Below are the choices available.

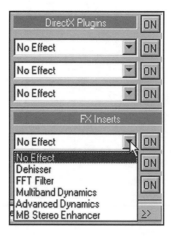

In this shot, I selected Multiband Dynamics and clicked the ON switch. To the right of the ON switch is the Edit button. I click it once and get the Multiband Dynamics window.

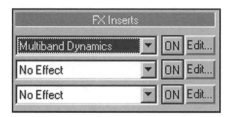

Here's the Multiband Dynamics Window.

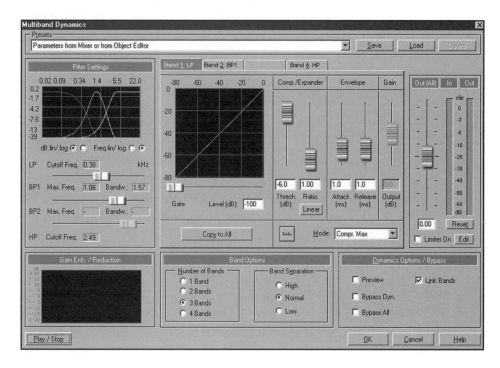

Position fades

This window lets you control the position of the object and how you fade into it or out of it.

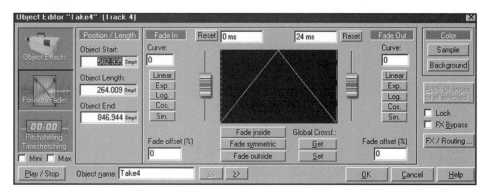

Pitch Shifting/Timestretching

This is the final section of the Object Editor where you change the pitch or stretch the time.

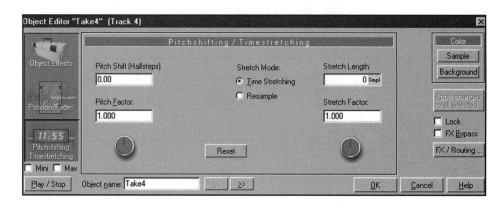

Object Editor summary

As you'll learn shortly, all effects and EQ are applied to a specific track in the mixer. This is true for all the major programs. But in Samplitude, not only can you assign effects to a track, you can select a specific audio file within the track (called an object) and independently to that object, and that object *alone*, apply EQ, reverb, effects, compression - whatever editing you feel it needs, *non-destructively* using plug-in effects packages. By non-destructive, we mean that you can apply an effect without changing the original audio file. So with Object Editor mixing, you do the mix within the track, not just the whole track. This is a major breakthrough that finally takes advantage of the computer's power to edit.

The main screen

Here's the main Samplitude screen using their demo Tutorial 1. What you're seeing are four tracks. To the left is the channel strip laid out within a square instead of a vertical strip.

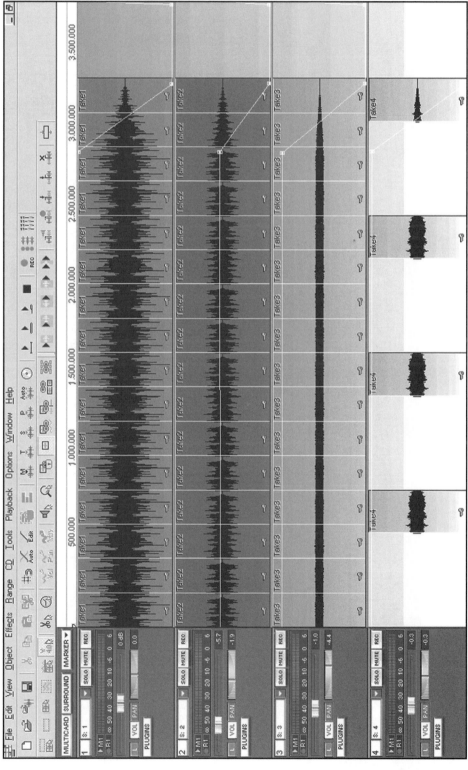

Where's the channel strip?

Mackie strip to the left, Samplitude below.

Notice that the channel strip is laid out in a more graphic manner and you also see the audio file you just recorded. A quick glance shows the solo, mute, volume, pan and record buttons. You'll also see above volume and pan, the meter lights for each channel strip.

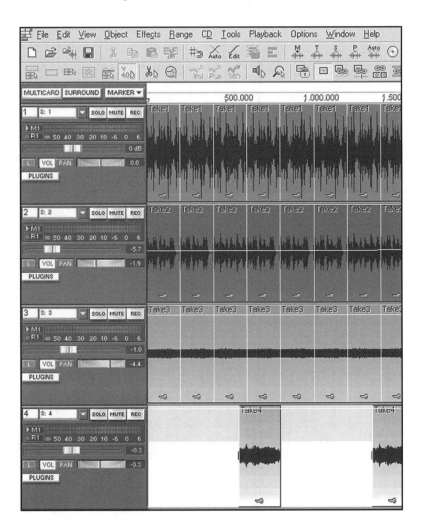

With Cubase and Emagic, you'll find that the virtual mixing board is all set up, ready to go. When you get into programs like Samplitude, Pro Tools or Vegas, you either "build" the virtual mixing board as you go, track by track, or you pre-create your board on opening (ideally, you'll create a master template from which to work). Below, is the setup menu for Samplitude as an example.

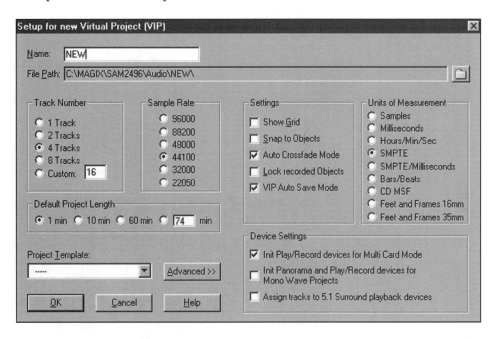

Looking at Samplitude's main screen, you don't see the EQ. That's because EQ in Samplitude is treated two ways:

1. There's either a 3-band or 5-band parametric EQ available for each track within Samplitude

3-band parametric EQ

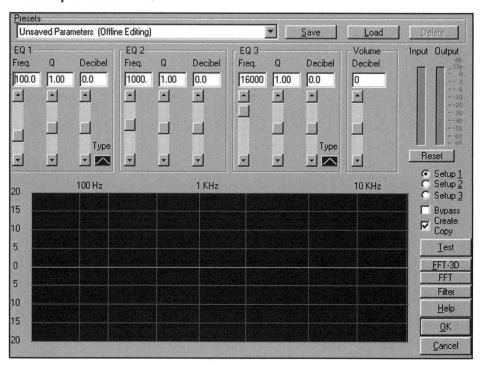

5-band parametric EQ

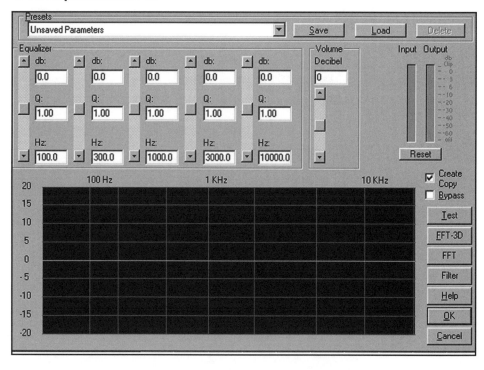

2. You have the option of using a separate DirectX EQ plug-in. Here's the TC Works Native Essentials 3-band parametric EQ.

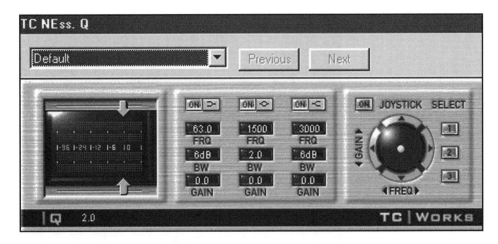

Also, you can set up volume or pan curves. Here's a volume curve.

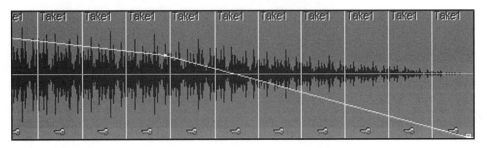

Using the mouse, you can draw in specific volume or pan changes. This is a mouse drawn volume change.

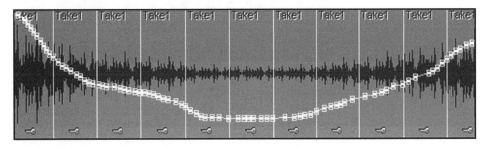

The Samplitude virtual mixing board

We'll look at this in more detail when we study signal flow, but for now notice how close it follows the design of the Mackie channel strip.

Why you'd want a complementing program

If you're already using a sequencing/digital audio program, why would you want Samplitude? There are four answers.

1. **Once you've finished your work, you still need to master it and burn a Red Book standard CD.** Burning to Red Book standard insures that your CD can be played on other CD players. Well, you can both master and burn the CD within Samplitude and as a bonus, you can continue to work while you're burning the CD. Plus, you get a powerful audio editor and multitrack recording program.

2. **Because there is such fierce competition among sequencing/digital audio companies, updates are frequent, and at times unstable.** In one major program alone in the course of a year, we had stuttering, digital audio bursts at the end of a recorded audio track, and an audio driver change that neutralized the audio cards for many users. A professional can't afford this. That's why in our studios we sequence in one program and record into Samplitude.

3. **Because of extended use of virtual synths and samplers within the host programs.** Virtual synths and samplers extend the range of your programs in powerful ways. However, to take full advantage of that power, you need an audio card with lots of outs to assign virtual instruments to their own channels. For speed recording, it's faster to record synths, samplers and virtual instruments to an external recording program like Samplitude than to fight the routing issues to record within the host computer.

4. **Playing to the greatest strengths of the programs you use**. One program is great for sequencing. Another is outstanding for multitrack recording. A third program could be what you need for sampling. By playing to the strengths of each type of program, you end up with the most professional sounding results.

5. **It sounds better.** I won't win friends at the other software companies on this one, but when you record the same example in all the other programs and then in Samplitude, your ears will tell you that it sounds better. We ran that test and were astonished to hear the aural difference.

For recording without MIDI sequencing

I don't think this program can be beat. It does everything brilliantly. If it had more than a basic MIDI sequencing program, everyone else on the block would be nervous. That's how solid this program is.

One concern on effects

Samplitude is a powerful program and it comes with many internal plug-ins. However, you will need an extra set of effects plug-ins. That's because some of the effects within Samplitude are applied directly to the audio file. This is called destructive editing. Instead, you want effects (reverb, etc.) that you can apply that are "real time" but don't affect the actual file. There are many great effects like TC Works Native Bundle, Waves, and Arboretum Hyperprism.

Section Wrap Up

To conclude, we've looked at what a studio is. A studio has a control room and a studio area. Those are the two main parts. In home recording, the room you record in doubles as both control room and studio. Portable units contain both the mixing board and the recorder. Advanced digital units contain the recorder, mixing board, effects, and CD mastering and burning capabilities. They're also portable.

By comparison, software programs running in computers are more fixed in place. Generally, the audio card within the computer is connected to either an analog or digital mixing board. One does not "drag" a computer and mixing board easily from room to room! Thus, the room in which you have your computer and mixing board is also a dual control room and studio.

Programs like Cakewalk, Cubase, Emagic, Performer and Samplitude are professional programs, value priced so that most any customer could buy them. These programs come with sequencer, digital audio recorder, virtual mixing boards, plug-ins (effects) and in some cases, with musical notation. Like the portable digital units, they represent within the software the broad contents of a control room. However, unlike the portable digital units, software programs require an audio card for recording and connection to a mixing board. It's possible, in some cases, to bypass the mixing board and record direct into an audio card, but this is not often successful.

Where's the channel strip?

We looked at the channel strip of a Mackie board and compared it to the channel strips of an analog unit, two digital units and software. We learned that if you can run the channel strip, you can largely run the mixing board.

When asking, "Where's the channel strip?" we saw that the analog unit was a smaller set of the larger board, but that the digital units implement the concept of the channel strip. As such, to learn a digital unit or virtual program, one most know the parts of the channel strip, what they do, and how they work. From there, you ask the question, "Where's the channel strip?" Its answer guides you in how to operate the program.

Asking this question also helps us to understand how to work both the hardware and the software, which borrows features and terms from the hardware but repackaged to fit within one or two monitor screens.

Note

All of the software programs have been used to create scores for movies for theatrical release. With the exception of the high end Pro Tools systems, there is no longer a line between amateur and professional software. The line between the amateur and the professional is that of patience and acquired skill with a meaningful end result - the mastered CD.

However, this overview is but our first step. Inside the studio are all kinds of equipment and cables. So the next group of chapters will look at these along with how to connect to the mixing board. As we learn how to connect to the mixing board, using our Mackie 32-8 bus board as a model, we'll also learn a concept called signal flow. And everything you learn can be applied to every mixing board or software program you'll ever use.

The room you record in

By looking at studio sizes, you learned that a studio has to have room to record. By contrast, in a home situation, you're spending a lot of time looking for a spot or place within the room to record in. A smaller digital or analog unit is portable, so you can take it anyplace. But with a virtual studio you operate in a fixed environment.

And here a great deal of procedural planning is needed. When it's just you, it's no problem. When you bring in others, then you have to start thinking about mics and mic stands, cables, how you'll coordinate a count off so that everyone is playing together, how you'll isolate sound so that the performance in one room won't spill over into the mic in the other room, etc.

There are lots of variables. Panic sets in when these variables aren't considered and everyone is standing around staring at *you*.

What you can now do...

If you've paid attention to our question, "Where's the channel strip?" you should now be able to approach almost any analog or digital mixing board and with confidence look for the fader, mute, solo, pan, EQ section, and aux section. Now, we have lots more to learn, but this is the foundation from which we'll build.

The next section

Our next section looks at jacks and cables, connectors on the back of analog and digital units, connectors on amps, direct boxes, et al, and how to connect everything to the board so you can get *sound*. We'll finish it by looking at how computers connect to both analog and digital boards.

Connectors and Cables - Part 1

In this section we start looking at the "things" that connect to the back of a mixing board or into the audio card of a computer. This may seem like a silly place to start until you consider standard terms like lightpipe cable, Centronics connector, XLRs, RCAs, tip ring sleeve, balanced, and so on. Just understanding how to do a "simple" connection can be a nightmare if you don't understand what the cables are and the connectors that go with them. To make my teaching point, kindly study the following diagrams:

Back of the Tascam

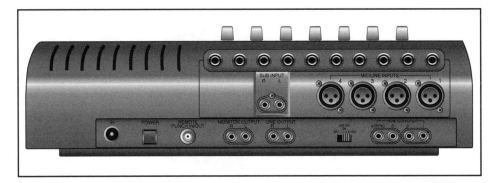

Back of the BR-8

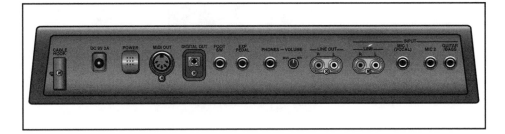

Back of the VS-1880

Notice how many different connectors are needed for each kind of unit, from the Tascam to the VS-1880. And just for the VS-1880, separate from the power cable and parallel port, *six* different connector types are needed. By comparison, for the Mackie to the right, as an analog mixing board, only three types of connectors are needed.

Insert section of the Mackie board

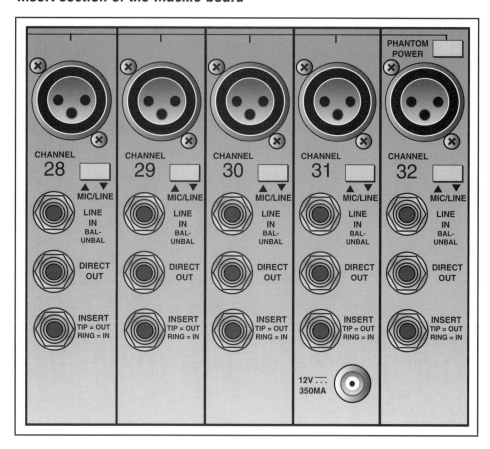

Master section of the Mackie board

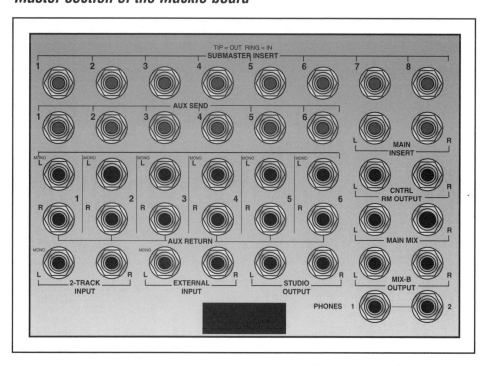

Connection observations

1. Whether analog or digital, the same "basic" connectors and cables are used from unit to unit.

2. Each unit can require three or more different types of cables.

"Things" that connect to mixing boards (small or big!)

It's really a fairly short list, but let's go through it anyway.

1. Mics (microphones)

2. Synths and Samplers

3. Guitars and Basses (electric or acoustic, depending on whether the acoustic ones have a pickup inside them).

4. External effects units

5. Recorders

6. AD/DA converters

7. Audio cards from computers

8. Power amps (to run the speakers)

9. Powered speakers

10. MIDI cables (mostly for portable digital units)

11. ADATs

12. Audio patchbay

7 connectors for audio

When we sum all this up, there are 7 main connectors used in different configurations to connect to a mixing board or to other gear. The illustrations on the page opposite are modeled after Hosa Technology cables.

RCA (Analog)

Guitar or Mono 1/4" (Tip Sleeve)

Stereo (Tip Ring Sleeve)/Balanced

XLR or AES/EBU (Analog or Digital)

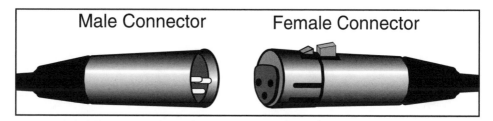

Male Connector Female Connector

ADAT Optical TOSLink

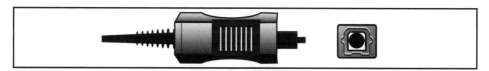

S/PDIF Coaxial RCA (Digital)

Neutrik Speakon

Cable combinations

There are many cable configurations, but here are the most common.

RCAs

Originally created by the Radio Corporation of America (hence, RCAs). These are also called phono connectors, and they're unbalanced. RCAs are mostly used in home recording and stereo gear, however they can be used in the studio depending on the equipment.

RCA - RCA

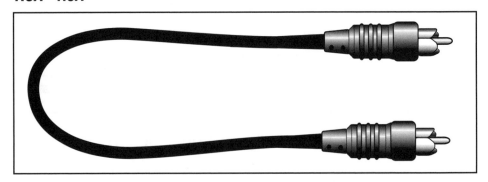

RCA - 1/4" mono

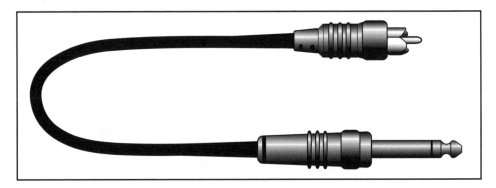

RCA to XLR male or female (this is a newer configuration available from Hosa Technology).

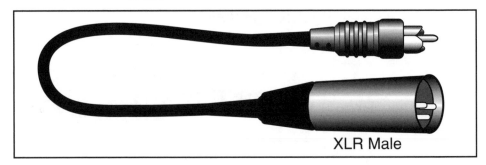

XLR Male

1/4" TS

TS stands for Tip Sleeve. This is an unbalanced cable. These are your standard "guitar" cables that connect from the guitar to the power amp, to effects boxes or directly to the mixing board. They can also be used to connect synths and samplers to the mixing board. With synths and samplers, and any other equipment, check the manual to determine if 1/4" balanced cables are needed instead.

1/4" to 1/4"

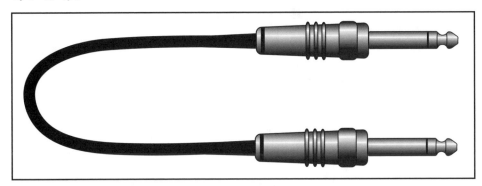

1/4" to RCA

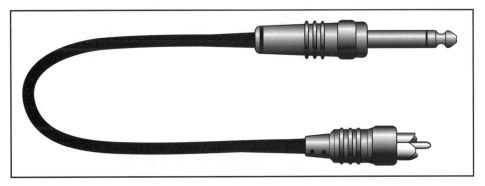

1/4" to XLR male or female*

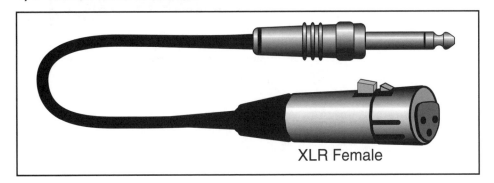

XLR Female

*These are unbalanced.

1/4" balanced (Tip Ring Sleeve), also called 1/4" stereo

I'll explain what balanced means shortly. These are the cables most often used to connect to a mixing board. Units requiring these cables will tell you either on the box or in the manual. The T (tip) is left. R (ring) is right. The S (shield) is the ground. It's a balanced interconnect with the positive and negative lines tied to the T (left) and R (right) respectively. S acts as an overall shield (Source: Rane Online Reference Guide).

- audio cards to AD/DAs

- audio cards directly to the board

- effects boxes to the board

- samplers and synths to the board

1/4" balanced to 1/4" balanced

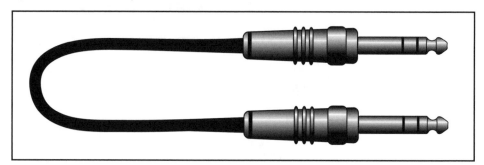

*1/4" balanced to XLR (various configurations)***

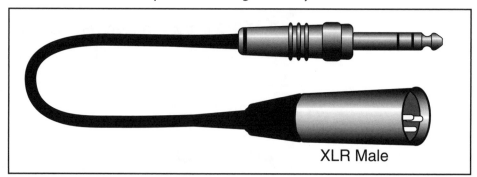

XLR Male

** These are balanced.

XLR

For a detailed history of the XLR, see the Rane Online Reference Guide. This is the standard connector for digital and analog balanced line interconnect between audio equipment. XLRs are often found mated with a 1/4" cable to connect a mic to the mixing board. Depending on the mixing board, you'll either connect the mic to the mic/line input with a 1/4" cable or to the back of the board with an XLR connector on the end. Most often it's a female XLR connecting to the mic with the 1/4" or male XLR on the other end. Remember, when a 1/4" connects to an XLR it can be balanced or unbalanced. You must specify which one you need.

XLR male to XLR male

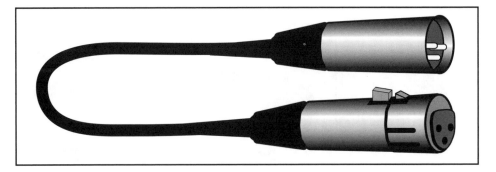

XLR male to XLR female

XLR male to 1/4"

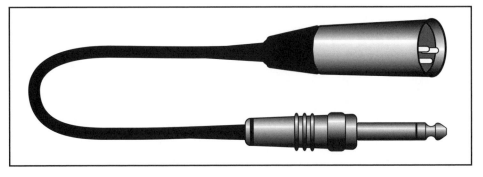

XLR male to RCA

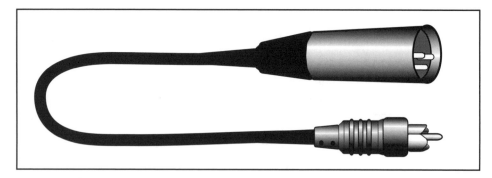

XLR female to 1/4"

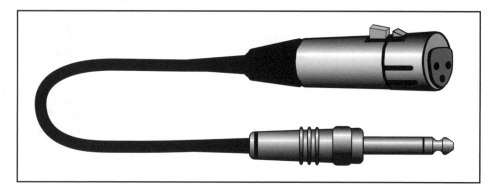

XLR female to RCA

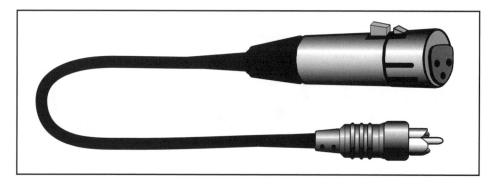

ADAT Optical Lightpipe/TOSLink

The Rane Reference Guide defines TOSLink (Toshiba Link) as, "A popular consumer equipment fiber optic interface based upon the S/PDIF protocol, using an implementation first developed by Toshiba." So the ADAT optical users a fiber optic cable and interface over which it carries audio signals. S/PDIF is an acronym for SONY/PHILLIPS Digital Interface. There are two different fiber optic cable connectors. The one shown below is the most common.

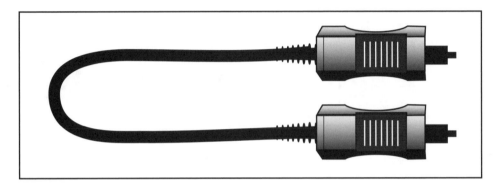

S/PDIF Coaxial RCA

This is an all digital connection using an RCA connector. As mentioned above, S/PDIF is an acronym for SONY/PHILLIPS Digital Interface. The Rane Reference Guide defines a coaxial cable as "a single copper conductor, surrounded with a heavy layer of insulation covered by a thick surrounding copper shield and jacket. A constant-impedance unbalanced transmission line."

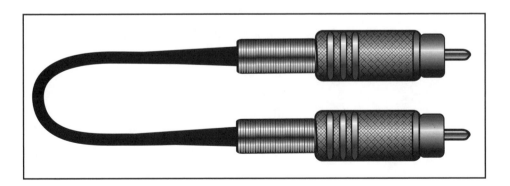

Neutrik Speakon

Originally designed by Neutrik, the Neutrik brand of Speakon cables are recognized as the Industry standard. They're used as loudspeaker amplifier connectors and come in 2, 4, and 8 pole contact versions. Some equipment uses Speakon connectors with only one pin-set wired. You'll need to check your equipment manuals to make sure. Speakons can be found in both single and multi-channel configurations depending on your application. Connectors typically found on the other end are 1/4" Phone or dual banana plugs.

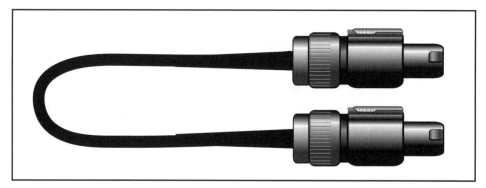

Balanced cables

From the Rane Online Reference Guide:

> "The IEEE dictionary defines a balanced circuit as, "a circuit in which two branches are electrically alike and symmetrical with respect to a common reference point, usually ground." This is the essence of a balanced interconnect. Namely, that two lines are driven equally and oppositely with respect to ground. Normally this also implies that the receiving circuits have matching impedances. Exactly matching impedances is preferred for it provides the best common mode rejection. Balanced lines are the preferred method (for hum free) interconnecting of sound systems using a shielded twisted-pair. Because of its superior noise immunity, balanced lines also find use in interconnecting data signals, e.g., RS-422, and digital audio, e.g., AES/EBU. The principal behind balanced lines is that the signal is transmitted over one wire and received back on another wire."

Simply put, balanced cables give a cleaner signal and often eliminate system hums.

Cable adapters

This chapter wouldn't be complete without discussing cable adapters. There are two broad uses for cable adapters:

1. to make a longer cable out of two

2. to transform one type of connector into another to create a common fit. For example, you'll find adapters for RCAs that let them connect to 1/4", etc.

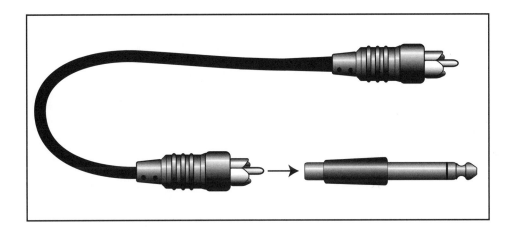

But how do these cables connect to the board?

That's next.

12 Connecting to the Tascam

In these next few chapters we're going to look at what connectors connect to each input on the board, and what types of cables connect to each connector. For example, you'll identify one connection possibility as a 1/4" mono. But what connectors can be at the end of that cable? For the correct answers, you'll have to look back at Chapter 11. Starting hint - this unit has no digital cables.

Please see illustration on next page.

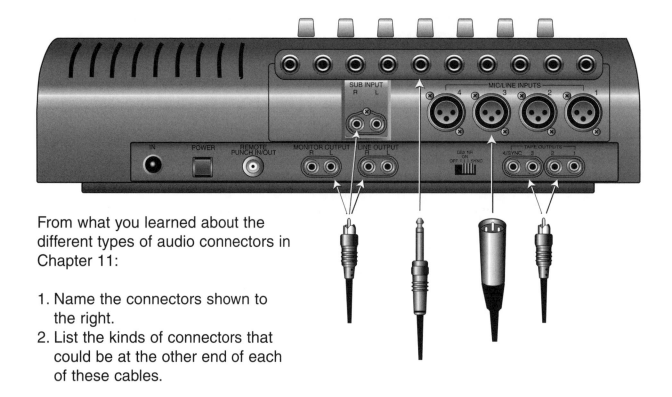

From what you learned about the different types of audio connectors in Chapter 11:

1. Name the connectors shown to the right.
2. List the kinds of connectors that could be at the other end of each of these cables.

Connecting to the Roland BR-8

The Roland BR-8 is a digital recorder. But a quick look on the back of the Roland BR-8 tells us that this unit uses a combination of audio cables plus one MIDI cable. Because MIDI isn't audio, we haven't discussed that cable yet. We'll simply acknowledge that it exists. As before, identify the cable connectors and types of cables that could possibly be used.

Please see illustration on next page.

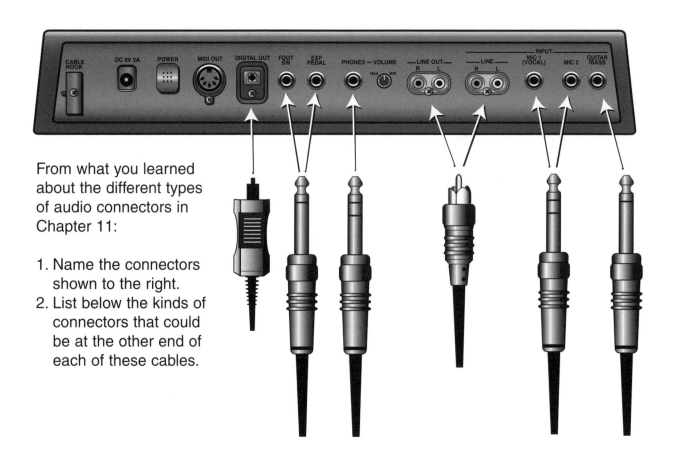

From what you learned about the different types of audio connectors in Chapter 11:

1. Name the connectors shown to the right.
2. List below the kinds of connectors that could be at the other end of each of these cables.

14
Connecting to the Roland VS-1880

With the Roland VS-1880, we have a digital unit that uses a majority of the connector types studied so far. As with the previous two chapters, identify each type of cable connector you see, and then which types of cables might connect there. The principles that you learn here, we'll then next apply to connectors and cables that connect to "things" which then connect to the mixing board. Once that section is concluded, our next steps will be to understand the signal flow of an analog board.

Please see illustration on next page.

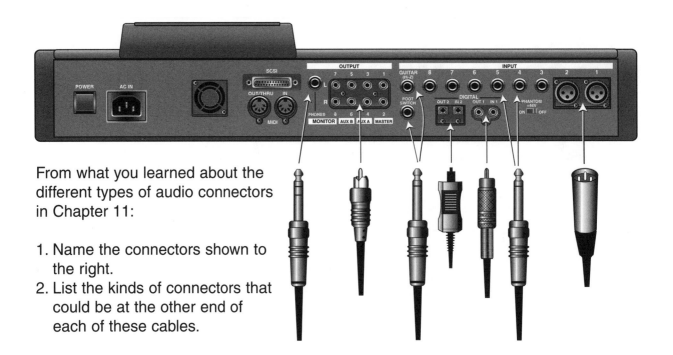

From what you learned about the different types of audio connectors in Chapter 11:

1. Name the connectors shown to the right.
2. List the kinds of connectors that could be at the other end of each of these cables.

Connectors & Cables Part 2: "Things" they connect to

Now that we've learned the cable connectors and various cable configurations of what can connect to the mixing board, we go to the next step and look at various musical instruments and pieces of equipment needing the various cables to connect to.

Connection list

Here's a starting list:

- Amps: bass, guitar, and keyboard
- Electric guitars
- Electric bass guitars
- Direct boxes
- Mic preamps
- Professional microphones
- Synthesizers
- Samplers
- Power amps
- Computer audio cards
- AD/DA converters
- Effects boxes
- Powered (active) monitors
- Headphones
- External compressor/limiters
- Boomboxes/portable units
- Foot pedal
- Expression pedal

So let's look at each of these pieces found in most studios to understand the connector/cable dynamics each represents. Once we understand this, our next step is to learn how to connect these pieces, with the right cables, to the mixing board. To learn this, we'll start with the larger Mackie 32-8 bus mixing board and work our way down to the smaller analog and digital units. *This approach lets you learn signal flow on the larger board and then to see how it's applied to the smaller "personal" units.* From this point, we're in prime position to understand the dynamics of how to add a computer with a sequencing/digital audio program into the recording/mixing environment.

Amps

There are three types of amps: guitar, bass, and to a limited degree, a keyboard amp, since keyboard amps for synths and samplers are most often used in live performance situations. Amps come with volume controls and basic tone controls (3-band EQ) labeled low, mid and high. Less expensive amps will only have one tone control. How the EQ is set up is different with each manufacturer. For example, Peavey (www.peavey.com) has basic 3-band EQs on their guitar amps, but 7-band EQs on their higher end bass models. Peavey keyboard amps have an EQ section and reverb.

Amp configurations

There are two basic types of configurations:

- amp only
- amp head and separate speaker cabinet

Note:

Throughout this book, most of our amp examples come from Peavey (www.peavey.com) because of all the Internet sites we vistited, Peavey gave the most customer support and information of any other amp manufacturer. Therefore, I am pleased to feature them.

Amp only

You can buy an amp that's just an amp, meaning you connect to it with an electric instrument or mic (or both if designed that way) and operate it solely with the basic volume and fundamental tone controls.

Amp & Compressor

You can get an amp that also has a compressor with it. The purpose of a compressor is to help shape the sound by "evening out" extreme highs and lows in volume. This is an oversimplified explanation, but for now, just understand that the addition of a compressor allows the player to shape his total performance style within the amp.

Amp & Compressor & EQ

This is the next step in sound shaping because here you have volume, compressor and EQ. This EQ is beyond the standard low/mid/high tone controls often appearing as a 7-band EQ (Peavey). Earlier you saw a screen shot from Cubase showing the compressor and EQ built into each channel strip. Well, the same concept applies here.

Amp & Compressor & EQ & Reverb!

This is the ultimate for an artist to shape their live sound - four key effects units within a single amp. The average price range of a quality amp is from $250 to $1200 US. The price of quality separate components (compressor, EQ and effects unit) can range from $250 - $5,000 *each*. So a combination system, while appearing to be very expensive, is really a seriously value priced unit, placing in one system what many could never be able to afford otherwise.

About Music and Sound

Music is all about sound and expression. Every professional artist seeks to have his own unique sound that separates him from other players. This sound is created by performance and creative skill, but also for "electric" or "electronic" players, with the added element of "tone controls" to add a new dimension of sound shaping and expression to their playing. This means that a player can achieve a particular style to his playing through the judicious use of his amp system.

At first, this is a live performance issue. However, once the sound (or style) is achieved, the next step is to capture that sound coming through the amp system into a recording.

This is the second phase of experimentation. Having achieved a "live" sound, this next step searches for the right mic(s) and recording techniques needed to faithfully capture that sound.

However, this also works in the reverse! You've created a recorded sound in your studio that you must now determine how to deploy in a live situation!

Or you want to create a "studio sound" that will only remain a studio sound since a live stage presentation might not capture the fullness of sound achieved in the studio. Just remember that sound, like beauty, is in the ear of the beholder.

Amp head and speaker cabinet (also called "enclosures")

The same considerations that exist with amp "combo" or combination units also exist with the selection of amp heads and separate speaker systems. The amp head is most often called "the amplifier" or "the head." Here, we have a component parts approach to assembling a performer's style. This means you can mix'n' match heads and cabinets between different manufacturers. "Heads" are available by the same types of features: basic + compressor + EQ + reverb.

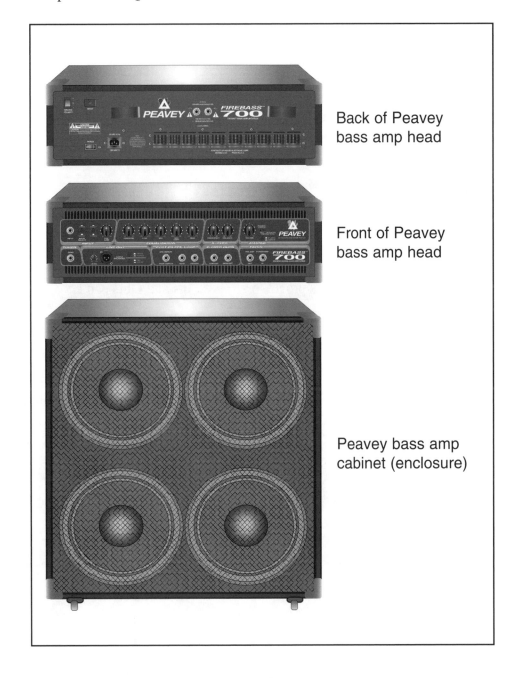

Back of Peavey
bass amp head

Front of Peavey
bass amp head

Peavey bass amp
cabinet (enclosure)

Inputs & Outputs

Some amps have inputs only. This means you can connect your instrument only, possibly a second instrument or a mic. Inputs can be:

- a 1/4" connector mono
- a 1/4" TRS for a mic
- an XLR balanced for a mic

Recording Point

If the amp only has inputs, you can only record the sound by miking the amp. More on this later in the book.

Some amps have outputs which enable you to connect directly to a mixing board. Here you'll have to determine which sound you like better: the direct sound or the miked amp sound. Outputs can be:

- a 1/4" connector mono
- a 1/4" TRS for a mic
- an XLR balanced for a mic

Some amps have Sends (out!) and Returns (In!) so that you can add outside effects processors. These Ins and Outs can be:

- a 1/4" connector mono
- a 1/4" TRS for a mic
- an XLR balanced

Here's a model from Peavey to illustrate these points:

Solid State or Tube or Both?

Besides the aforementioned features, amps are also available as solid state, tube, and a hybrid.

Solid State

This is an all electronic construction.

Tube amps

These amps are built around vacuum tubes. They're more highly sought after because of the "warmer" sound they give.

Hybrid

Has a tube preamp and the rest is solid state.

Open or closed back?

Amps are either open back or closed back.

Open back

Most combo amps are open-backed, meaning that there's no covering on the back side of the cabinet. Here, the sound escapes through the back of the amp. Some feel this gives a more "open" sound.

Closed back

Here, the back of the amp is covered. Some feel you get a more "punchy" sound this way since all the bass frequencies are pushed out the front, whereas with the open back, they come out the back.

Electric guitars

Electric guitars have a 1/4" connector. These are most often mono so only a 1/4" TS is needed. However, some electric guitars allow for balanced cables (1/4" TRS) to create a stereo effect through amps that allow for mono or stereo settings.

3 Basic kinds of electric guitars

These are:

- the hollowbody
- the semi-hollowbody
- the solidbody

What makes an electric guitar

This guitar has a pickup (microphone!) inside that produces a sound different than a miked acoustic guitar.

The Hollowbody

Often used by jazz guitarists. It's called a hollowbody because like an acoustic guitar, it's hollow on the inside. These are considered the best, of all electric guitar types, for playing fingerstyle.

The Semi-Hollowbody

The favorite of blues players, jazz-rock players and others. This guitar, like its name suggests, is also hollow, but thinner, thus having less resonance.

Solidbody

This type, which represents the majority of electric guitars, includes Stratocasters, Les Pauls, Telecasters, and others. Manufacturers in this area include Dean, Ibanez, Jackson, Paul Reed Smith, Steinburger and others. Each type also has its own sound. A Les Paul is different from a Strat is different *from...* There are distinct reasons why they're different which include the kind of pickup used, the pickup configuration, pickup wiring schemes and pickup controls.

More on recording electric guitars

As you can see, there are substantial issues involved with effectively recording guitar. This subject is covered in depth (200 pages!) by my colleague, Jon Chappell, and his excellent The Recording Guitarist available from Hal Leonard Corporation.

Bass guitars

Electric bass guitars have a 1/4" output connector. These are most often mono so only a 1/4" TS is needed. However, some electric basses allow for balanced cables to create a stereo effect through amps that allow for mono or stereo settings.

Three basic kinds of bass guitars

Unless custom made, bass guitars are solidbody. There are three basic types:

- standard (4 strings, bottom note E)
- fretless
- headless

Standard

This is a solidbody with 4 strings - E, A, D, G, with frets to position the fingers to perform each pitch or specific chords.

Fretless

This electric bass has four strings, too, but like its acoustic big brother, the contrabass, it too is fretless. Here, the performer learns to play by positioning his fingers as any violinist, violist, celloist or bassist would.

Headless

This is a fretted bass without the head on the end.

String configurations

Some electric basses have 5, 6, and 7 strings. The purpose of this is to extend the range of the bass down to the bottom B, a perfect 4th below the low E. An acoustic bass accomplishes this by the use of a bass extender which can lower the pitches down to C, or the additional of a fifth string. Since the electric bass can't accommodate a bass extender, an extra string is added, and in some cases, a modified design to allow for the extra strings.

Note:

Some bass players retune the five strings so that the bottom pitch is E and the highest string begins on C (E, A ,D, G, C).

6-Strings

Sometimes called a contrabass guitar. Strings are: B, E, A, D, G, C. Thus, the range is extended both in the lower and upper registers.

7-Strings

Manufactured by Conklin (www.conklinguitars.com). The pitches for each string are B, E, A, D, G, C, and F.

Direct boxes

This is a device that allows a musical instrument to be connected directly to the mic/line connector on the mixing board. It's purpose is to make electrical levels between the instrument and the mixing board match. Two types exist, tube and solid state.

Inputs & Outputs

Most often, direct boxes have 1/4" TS inputs and outputs with XLR balanced inputs and outputs. However, this depends on the individual unit.

Mic preamps

Preamp is short for preamplification. This box boosts the electrical signals so that levels from the mic to the mixing board match. Also, most come with a 48Volt Phantom Power switch to enable you to use condenser mics.

Inputs & Outputs

Varies with the manufacturer. Normally expect balanced XLR ins and outs. Some units also have 1/4" TS or 1/4" TRS for ins and outs. Price ranges from under $100 to several thousand dollars.

Professional mics

Illustrated below is the Shure SM57, the world's most popular mic. At the angle below, you'll see that the SM57 has an XLR Male connector within. This is true for most professional mics. Thus, an XLR Female balanced connector is required to connect.

Effects boxes

Reverb units, multieffects processors, compressors, etc., nearly always use 1/4" TRS for inputs and outputs, with a second option for XLR balanced inputs and outputs.Whether the XLR is present is subject to manufacturer design.

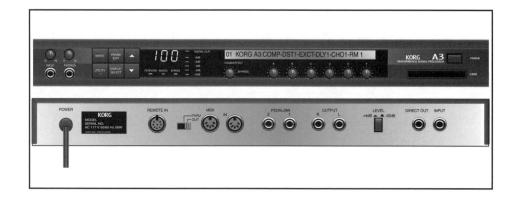

Synthesizers

Here's the back of an Alesis QS keyboard. Most synths have L/R Main connectors on the back. Some have 2 pairs, others have up to four pairs (Kurzweil). Unless otherwise stated by the manufacturer, these units take 1/4" TS cables.

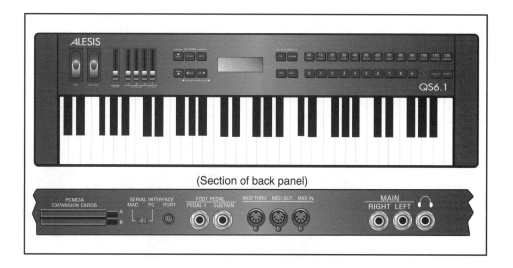

(Section of back panel)

Samplers

Professional samplers most often have balanced connections on the back. Depending on the company, this will be up to 8 1/4" TRS connectors on the back. These will be for inputs (for direct sampling) and output (for playback).

Professional power amps

For recording purposes, professional power amps are used to power the nearfield monitors (called passive speakers when they're not powered) that connect to the mixing board. Most often, monitors are connected with monitor cable attaching to clips on the back of the unit. Balanced output connectors then allow connection to the mixing board. Balanced output connectors are either 1/4" TRS or XLR. Power amps are measured with a figure called RMS. Depending on the speaker used, many studio systems operate at 100RMS per channel (also known as watts). When a power amp is described as being 200RMS this often means 100 watts per channel.

Powered (active) monitors

Powered active monitors are nearfield reference monitors that come with their own built in amplification. As such, a separate professional power amp isn't needed. Input connectors are 1/4" TRS and XLR.

Professional computer audio cards - analog

Professional audio cards record at 16-bit and above, whereas the typical computer sound card can be at 8-bit. Standard today is 24-bit. Professional audio cards have two portions. The first is the AD/DA converter card installed inside the computer. The second is the break out box that a cable from the computer card connects to. AD/DA converter is an acronym for a device that converts analog sound to digital (AD) and digital sound to analog (DA). When both are on the same card or within the same external unit (see section) it's called an AD/DA converter.

Break out box

The break out box normally has four or more 1/4" connectors for 1/4" TRS cables. Shown below is the MIDIMan M-Audio Delta 1010. This unit has 8 1/4" balanced connectors for audio inputs and 8 1/4" connectors for audio output.

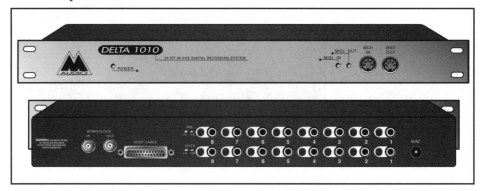

Note:

This subject is detailed in my book, *How MIDI Works* 6th Edition, published by Hal Leonard Corporation and in part within Windows. If you're a teacher K-12, please consider our accredited online class Introduction to MIDI and Digital Audio Recording. For details please see www. alexuniv.com.

Professional computer audio cards - Lightpipe

This is an audio card that uses fiber optics to transmit the audio signal. The audio card is inserted into the computer. The audio outs and audio ins are with TOSLink cables that connect directly to an AD/DA converter.

AD/DA converter

Pictured below is the RME ADI-8 Pro. This unit has audio ins and outs to and from the audio card using TOSLink cables. You then see 8 analog ins and 8 analog outs. These are all balanced connectors and so need 1/4" TRS cables to connect to the unit.

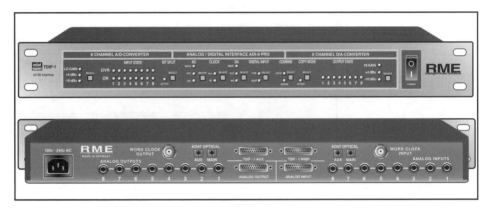

Headphones

Headphones have a 1/4" TRS connector. In Los Angeles, the most common headphones for post-production and recording are the AKG 240s.

Compressor/Limiter

Below is the Alesis 3630 Compressor Limiter with Gate. It uses 1/4" TS connectors for its Output and Input. The Side Chain connector uses a 1/4" TRS, where Tip = Return and Ring = Send.

Boomboxes/portable units

In simpler home set ups, keyboards are often connected to boomboxes, consumer power amps, or multipurpose amplifiers. These units take the RCA connector for all audio ins and outs.

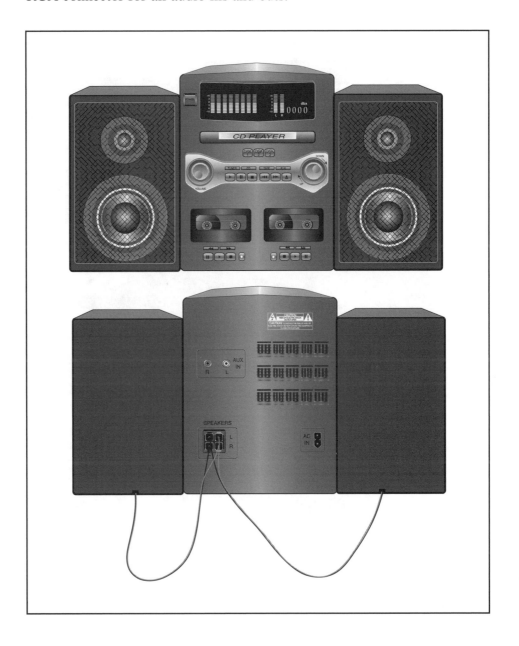

Foot pedal & Expression pedal

I'm mentioning foot and expression pedals here because some portable digital units, like the Roland BR-8, have inputs for them. These pedals use a 1/4" connector, but the cable and the connector are already manufactured with the pedal.

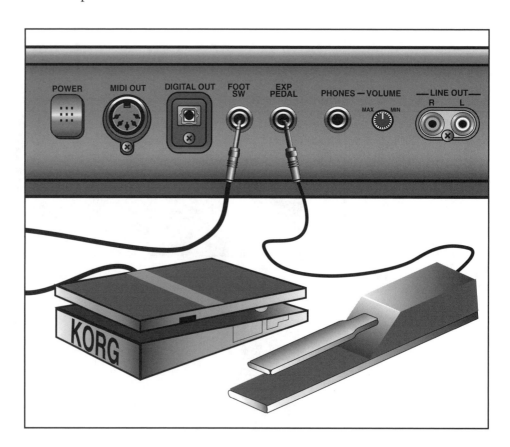

STOP!

Now that you know which connectors these units have, work out the cables each piece could potentially use. While this may seem silly, you'll be surprised as to the number of potential answers available depending on what mixing board or digital unit you're connecting to.

16 Connecting to the Larger Professional Analog Board - Part 1

Earlier I cited the engineer's rule of thumb: *If you can learn how to work one channel strip, you can understand how to run most of the board.* We're now about to apply this rule by learning how to connect to a larger analog mixing board using the Mackie 32-8 bus board as our model. While there are many excellent boards on the market, the Mackie is used in both smaller professional studios and professional project studios. It's an easy board to learn. So if you need to bring in an engineer to work on a project, chances are he'll have had some experience in using a Mackie board. Result: less time spent paying an engineer to learn your board.

Two halves of the channel strip

Throughout the opening chapters of this book I showed you the first half of the Mackie board. This was the actual channel strip housing the fader, pan, mute, solo, bus assignments, EQ, Auxes, and Trim (also called *gain* on some boards). What we didn't look at are the connector inputs and outputs directly above the channel strip. Now we're ready to.

To make this easier to learn, I've moved the illustration to the next page. So if you would kindly turn to it, we'll learn our next bit.

Top panel section

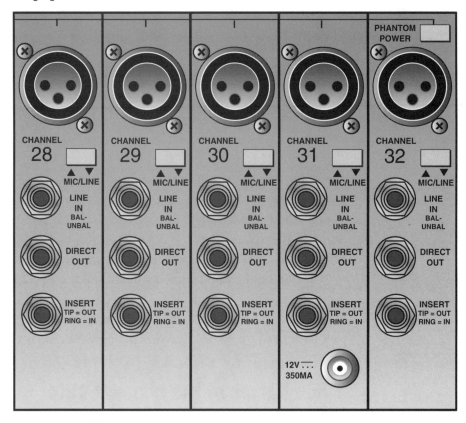

Let's start by defining what we see.

First there are five connectors. Three of them are 1/4", one is XLR and another is undefined. Let's go from the top *down*.

1. The XLR connector is an XLR F. It's balanced, and so needs an XLR cable with an XLR M connector on one end. The other end of the cable can be either a 1/4" TRS or another balanced XLR connector either M or F depending on what it's connecting to.

2. The next connector is labeled LINE IN and notice the extra labeling of BAL and UNBAL. This means that depending on what's being connected at this connector, it can be either a balanced or unbalanced 1/4" cable.

3. Direct Out takes either a BAL or UNBAL 1/4" cable. Direct Out lets you send whatever audio signal is coming into that specific channel strip out to say a tape player, audio card, etc.

4. Insert is also Channel Insert. This is where an effects unit is connected directly to affect the audio signal for that channel strip only. This is the connection point that enables you to build an effects chain with individual processors (ex. compressor + chorus + reverb) that's only applied at that specific channel strip.

5. The fifth connector is the surprise connector. It's for a light-bulb specific for the Mackie boards.

Phantom Power

Phantom Power is used to power condenser mics. On the Mackie board, one switch controls eight power strips. As such, one section of the board should be dedicated to mics needing Phantom Power. The connection steps are:

1. Connect the cable to the mic

2. Connect the mic to the XLR connector on the Mackie board

3. Press DOWN the Phantom Power switch

4. When finished recording, turn OFF Phantom Power. Tap the mic lightly to make sure it's off

5. Now disconnect the mic

Note

Do not plug a tube or ribbon type microphone into a channel strip where Phantom Power is turned on. However, you can connect a dynamic mic into the channel strip group where Phantom Power is turned on, usually with no problems.

Specific connection possibilities

Here I'm going to show the most common connection schemes for a channel strip on the Mackie board. Please note, that the connection information here is specific to the Mackie, *but largely applies to most boards*. You MUST CHECK your individual board's instructions and connectors to insure *correct connection and cables needed*.

Electric guitar/Electric bass

Basic connection patterns for the electric guitar or the electric bass are the same. Illustrations in this next section switch back and forth between guitar and bass.

Connecting the electric guitar to the board

The out of the electric guitar connects directly into the Mackie board. Use a 1/4" TS to 1/4" TS. Connect into the line input. Set switch to LINE. You can do this, but it's *not* recommended. The guitar has an extremely low output level, similar to that of a microphone, and does not really give a signal high enough for a line level input on the board.

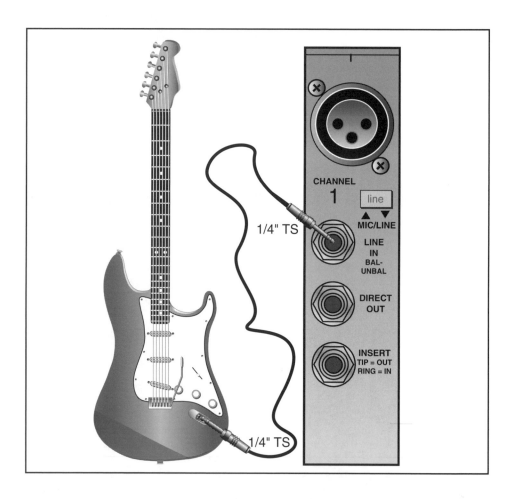

Connecting the electric guitar to a direct box (DI) then to the board

This is the preferred connection because the DI boosts the guitar's output level to match line level on the board. The cable connections depend on the DI. The DI can have:

- Unbalanced in to unbalanced out
- Unbalanced in to balanced out 1/4" TRS
- Unbalanced in to balanced out XLR

Unbalanced in to unbalanced out

This is a guitar with 1/4" TS connecting to the DI with a 1/4" TS coming from the DI into line in on the board. LINE is selected.

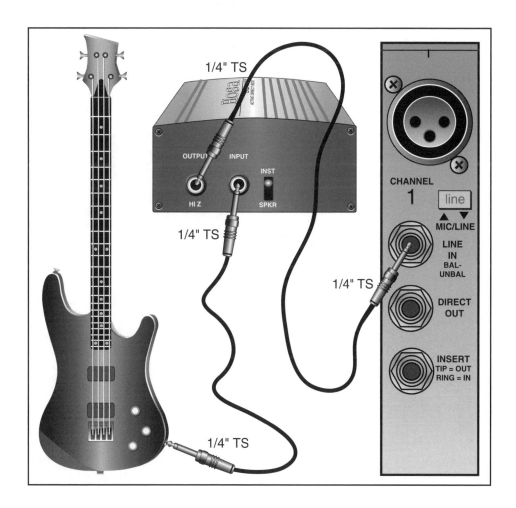

Unbalanced in to balanced out XLR

This is a guitar with 1/4" TS connecting to the DI with an XLR balanced from the DI into the XLR connector on the board. Here, the DI takes a high impedance unbalanced signal and turns it into a low impedance balanced signal that can be connected to a mic input. Set the Ground Lift switch on the DI box to Lift if you experience buzz, otherwise set it to Ground. MIC is selected on the Mackie board.

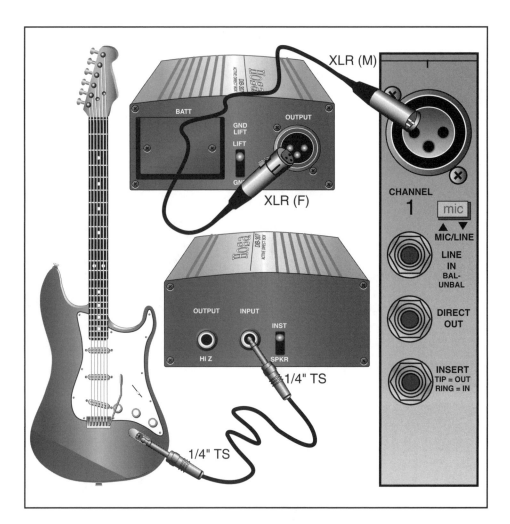

Note:

In this section, we've demonstrated direct boxes using the Hosa DIB 307. This is an excellent active DI, that's value priced. However, the applications shown in this section are particular to the DIB 307 and would not aply to a passive DI. Check the user manual of your DI for connections specific to your unit. You can find Hosa at www.hosatech.com.

Connecting the electric guitar and combo amp to the board

In the following diagrams we've chosen to show guitar amps made by Peavey. We chose Peavey because their web site had the clearest information about amps and their specifications. You can even download most of their amp manuals in PDF format to reference.

Peavey amps only use 1/4" TRS and XLR outputs to connect into a mixing board. Their 1/4" TRS output is labeled PREAMP OUT. Their XLR output is labeled LINE OUT. Note that amps by other manufacturers may use different terminology to connect to LINE IN on the board. Check the amp's manual if you're not sure.

WARNING! Check the amp FIRST to make sure that it:

- has an output

- has an output clearly labeled LINE OUT

If you DON'T see the words LINE OUT, and you can't find any instructions in the amp manual, go online to the amp maker and check the specs. If all else fails, call the amp's tech support company and ASK. A wrong connection here can potentially destroy your board. Cable connections depend on the amp. They can be

- unbalanced out 1/4" TS

- balanced out 1/4" TRS

- balanced out XLR

Unbalanced in to balanced out 1/4" TRS

This is a guitar with a 1/4" TS connecting to the amp with a 1/4" TRS coming from the preamp out on the amplifier into line in on the board. LINE is selected. If your amp has an unbalanced output, connect a 1/4" TS from line out on the amp to line in on the board.

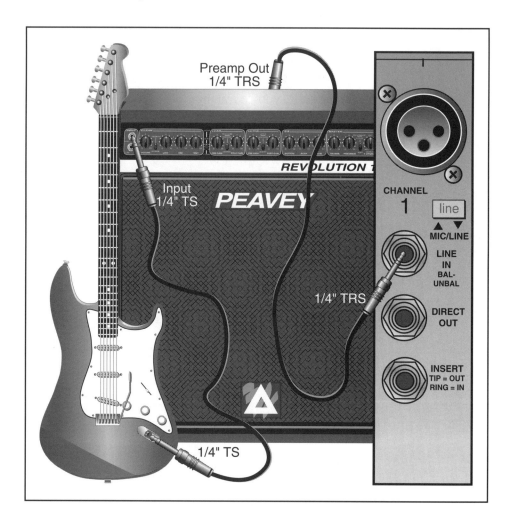

Unbalanced in to balanced out XLR

This is a guitar with 1/4" TS connecting to the amp with an XLR balanced from the amp into the XLR connector on the board. LINE is selected on the Mackie board.

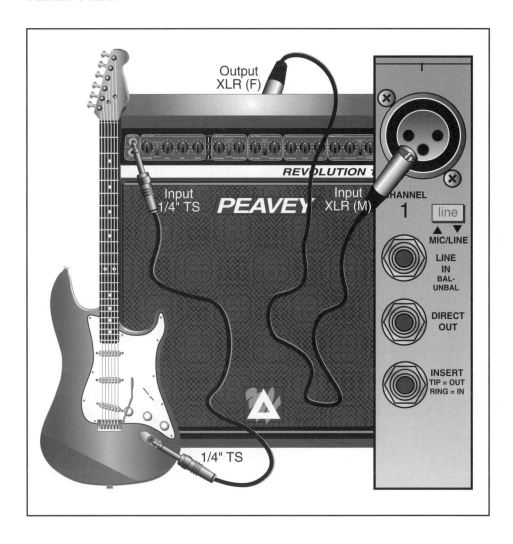

Connecting the electric bass guitar
and head/cabinet to the board

WARNING! Check the amp head FIRST to make sure that it:

- has an output

- has an output clearly labeled LINE OUT

If you DON'T see the words LINE OUT, and you can't find any instructions in the amp manual, go online to the amp maker and check the specs. If all else fails, call tech support for the amp company and ASK. A wrong connection here can potentially destroy your board. Cable connections depend on the amp head. They can be:

- unbalanced out

- balanced out 1/4" TRS

- balanced out XLR

Unbalanced in to balanced out 1/4" TRS

This is a guitar with 1/4" TS connecting to the amp head with a 1/4" TRS coming from the amp head's preamp out into line in on the board. LINE is selected. If your amp has an unbalanced output, connect a 1/4" TS from line out on the amp to line in on the board.

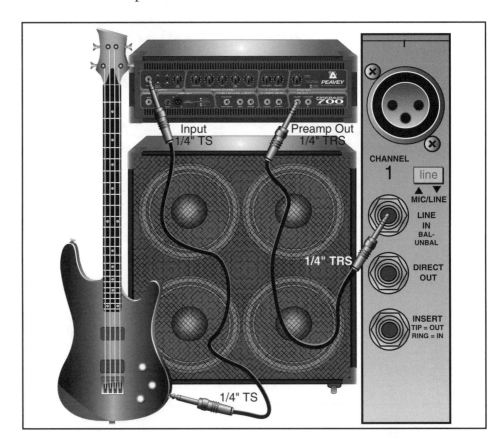

Unbalanced in to balanced out XLR

This is a guitar with 1/4" TS connecting to the amp with an XLR balanced from the amp head into the XLR connector on the board. LINE is selected on the Mackie board.

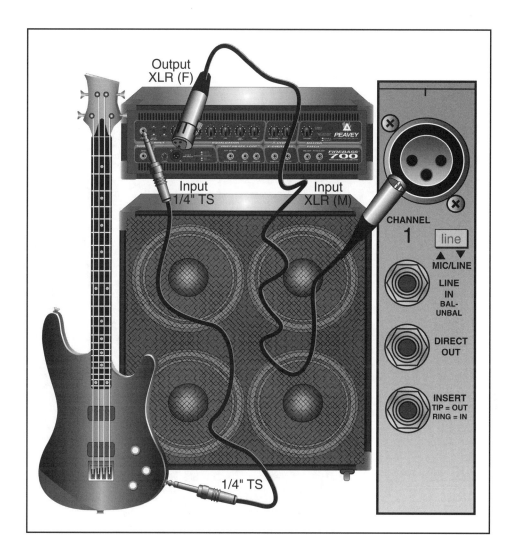

Connecting a synth to the mixing board

Most of the time the synth has 1/4" TS outs. Illustrated below is the back of an Alesis QS 6.1 keyboard. Thus, a 1/4" TS to 1/4" TS cable is used to connect to the line in on the board. The switch should be in the LINE position. You can connect a synth in either mono (usually labeled L/MONO) or in stereo with two cables.

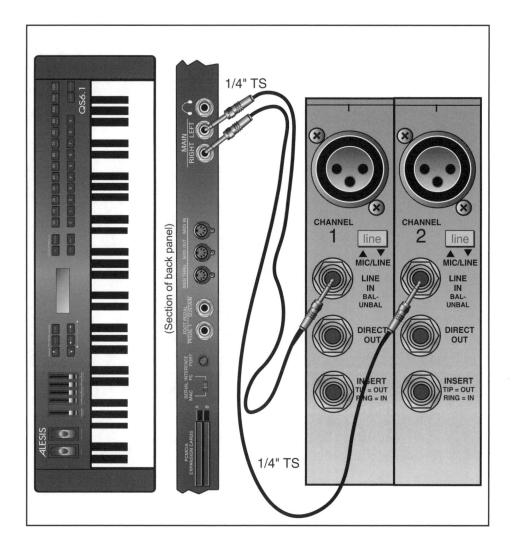

Connecting a sampler to the mixing board

High end professional samplers, including GigaStudio within a computer, most often suggest using 1/4" TRS - 1/4" TRS to connect from the sampler to the line in. The switch should be in the LINE position.

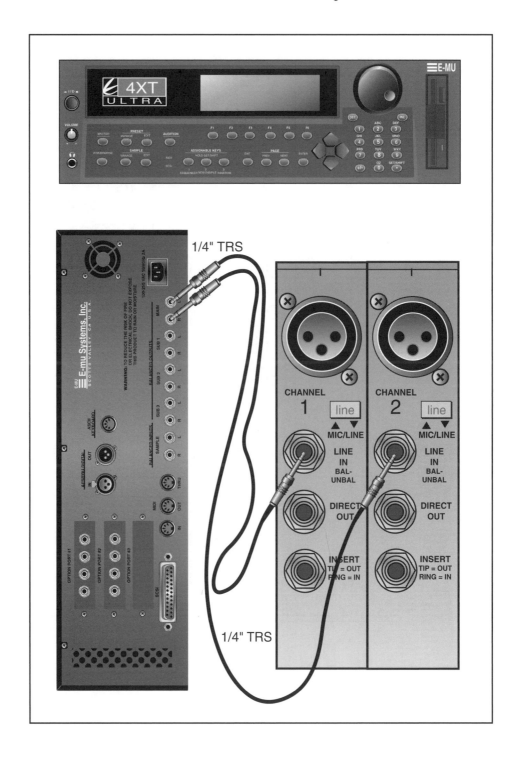

Connecting a softsampler to the board using the Alesis Lightpipe to AD/DA connection

Below is a full studio layout of GigaStudio connecting to the board using an RME Digi 9652 audio card to an Alesis AI3 AD/DA converter. Here, the outs from the AI3 connect to the Mackie board using 1/4" TRS to 1/4" TRS cables.

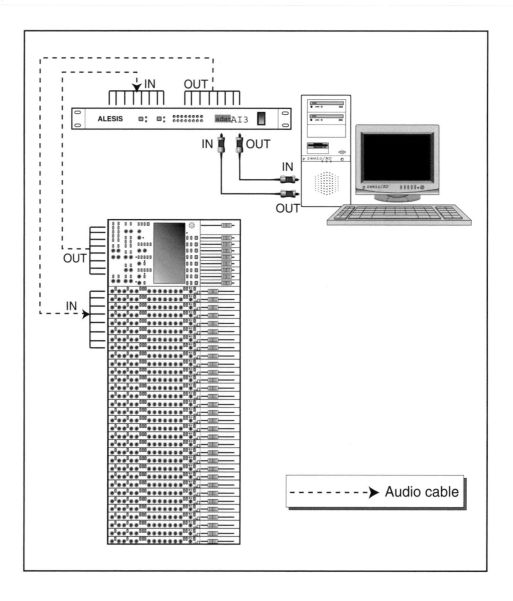

Connecting a multi-effects processor to the Insert connector

Earlier I spoke about connecting together a chain of effects processors that connect to the Insert connector on the board. You can do that with an individual group of effects processors, or you can buy what's called a multieffects processor that has each of these individual effects built into the one box. In our studio, we have two older units both created by Korg, the A1 and the A3 (you can still find these units on www.eBay.com with support available at www.aseries.org). OK, let's see two ways to connect using the multieffects processor.

Direct to the Insert connector

Connections can be for mono or stereo. Insert levels are controlled directly on the effects unit.

Mono

For mono, a special Y-cable is needed along with a stereo effects processor. The single connector goes to the Insert on the board. Then to Output (or Left Out) and Input (or Left In) accordingly on the effects unit.

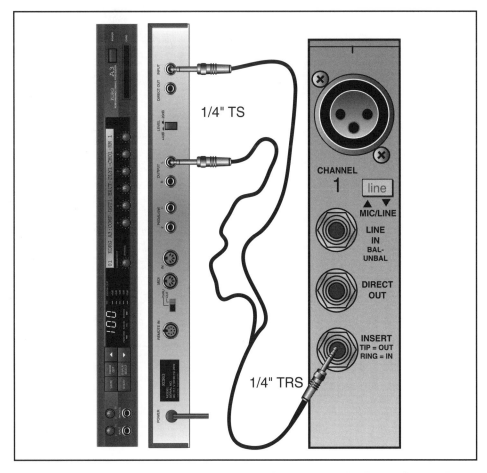

Stereo

For Stereo, a special Y-cable is needed along with a stereo effects processor. The single 1/4" TRS connector goes to the Insert on the board. Then to Left Out and Left In accordingly on the effects unit. Repeat the process on the adjacent channel strip going to Right Out and Right In on the effects unit.

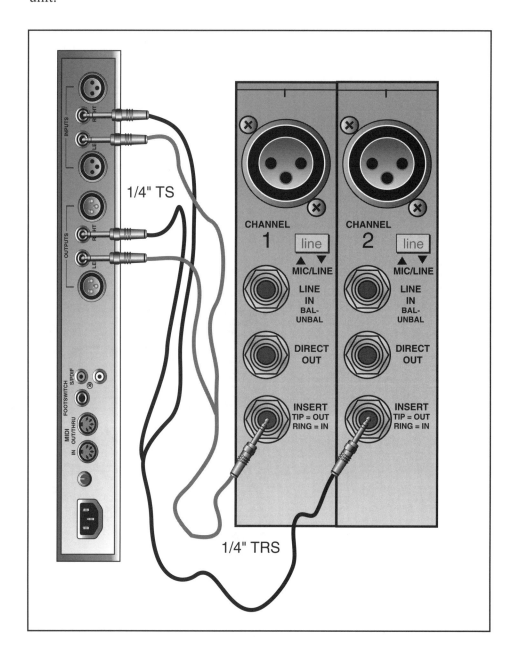

Connecting the electric guitar or bass
to the multieffects processor to the board

Connect the electric guitar or electric bass most often to the front panel of the unit then from the *outputs* of the unit to the *line in* of the board. Check the manual to determine if the outputs of the unit require 1/4" TS or 1/4" TRS for connecting to the board. If it's a stereo multieffects processor, connect to two adjacent channel strips at line in.

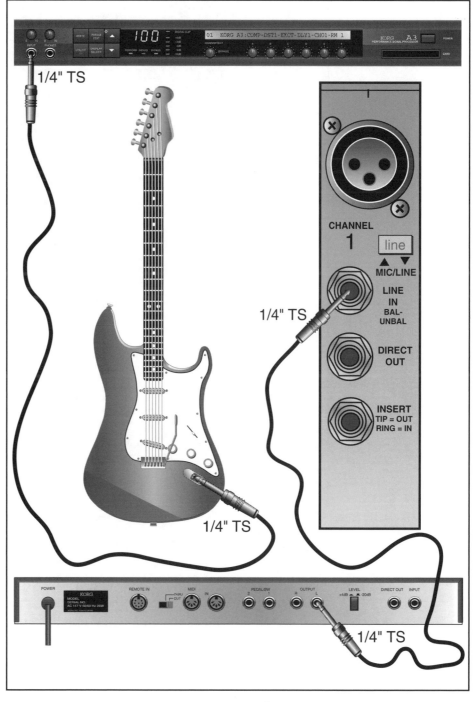

Connecting the electric guitar or bass to the amp to the multieffects processor to the mixing board

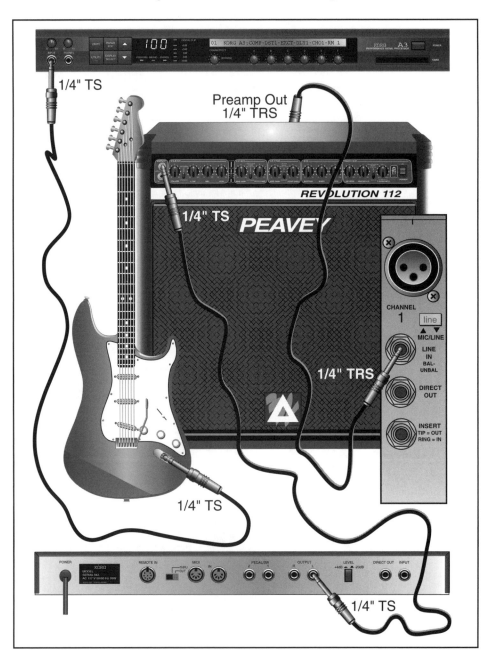

Using a 1/4" TS to 1/4" TS connect the output of the electric guitar or bass to the input on the multieffects unit. Connect the outputs of the unit to the appropriate inputs on the amp or amp head. Here you must check on both the effects unit and amp whether the connections are balanced or not. Then, connect the line out of the amp to the line in of the board, switch in LINE position. Here, the type of cable from amp line out to board line in depends on the amp.

Other combinations

You can do comparable set ups with keyboards connected to multieffects processors connected to an amp connected to a board. While not necessary, it can be done just to create a different sound.

Otherwise, the more common combination will be keyboard/sampler to multieffects processor to the board using the procedures covered in this chapter.

Settings Note

Multieffects processors often have settings on the back for --20dB for guitar amps and +4dB for professional mixing boards. Manufacturers suggest that when connecting to the board, first set the unit for -20dB. If the signal is too low, pull the faders all the way down, reset the unit for +4dB, then slowly raise the fader(s) to reset the volume levels. This procedure is covered later in the book with more detail.

What's next?

What I've given you in this chapter are the most common connection set ups to the mixing board. So next, we want to learn how to connect speakers and power amp to the mixing board.

Connecting to the Larger Professional Analog Board - Part 2: Monitors

In this chapter we learn how to connect two different types of monitors to the mixing board: passive and active. Passive monitors are the traditional approach requiring a professional power amp, speaker cable, and cables from the amp to the mixing board. Active monitors are self-powered, connect directly to the board, and have no need of a separate power amp. Later we'll cover monitors and monitor positioning. For now, just know that there are nearfield, midfield and farfield reference monitors. Most of the time you'll be working with nearfield monitors.

Parts list

Let's start with a parts list:

- Power amp and connections
- Speakers & Clips
- Speaker cable
- Mixing board and the connecting point

Power amp

Here's the generic back of a professional power amp. Here we have clips, 1/4" balanced connectors, and XLR balanced connectors. These connectors are INs.

Mixing Board connection point

This is the top of the Mackie board above the Master Control section. Look on the far right side for CNTRL RM OUTPUTS. This takes two 1/4" TRS cables that connect to the Ins of the power amp. Left to left, right to right. If the power amp has 1/4" connectors, then it's 1/4" TRS to 1/4" TRS. If the power amp has XLRs, then it's 1/4" TRS to XLR. OK, this is how the amp and board are connected. Now for the speakers.

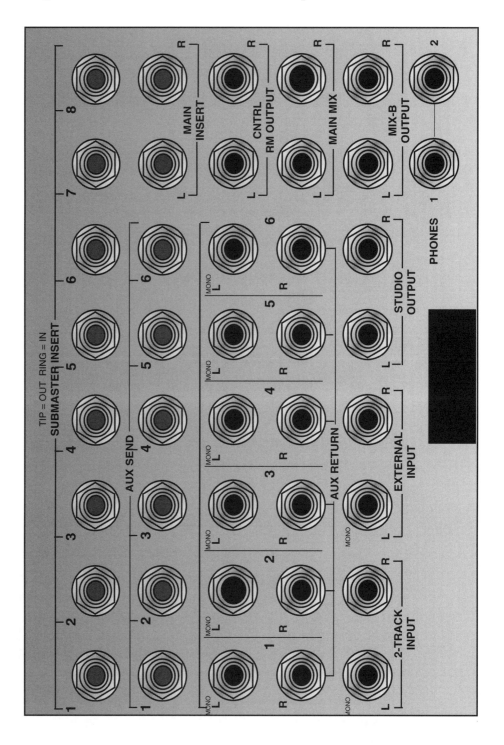

Connecting the speakers to the power amp

We'll discuss speaker cable next. Here we've attached speaker cable to one monitor. The smooth side can connect to the negative (black) and the ribbed side can connect to the positive (red). Since there's a left monitor and a right monitor, you connect the cables to the left and right of the power amp:

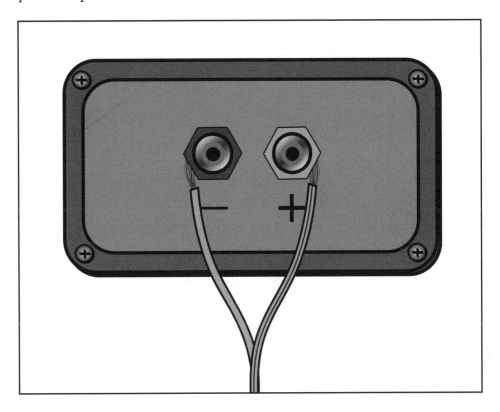

1. Left side: red from the speaker to red on the amp, black from the speaker to black on the amp.

2. Right side: red from the speaker to red on the amp, black from the speaker to black on the amp.

Note:

The left monitor is the left one facing you to your immediate left. The right monitor is the right one facing you to your immediate right. The amp will (normally) be clearly labeled L and R. Be very careful. This is a simple operation, because left and right positions on the amp are different from the way the monitors face you. The result is often temporary insanity as you sort it out. Be sure not to cross cable connections as this creates unwanted phase cancellation and can harm your speakers.

Nearfield monitor positioning

Whether with a smaller unit like the Roland BR-8 or the larger Mackie board, nearfield monitor positioning works the same way. Study the diagram below. Speakers are to be at "ear level" (also called *the sweet spot*) based on how high you sit in a chair. Ideally, they should be on speaker stands approximately 4' tall. Or they can sit on the ledge of the mixing board if it's wide and sturdy enough (or even exists!).

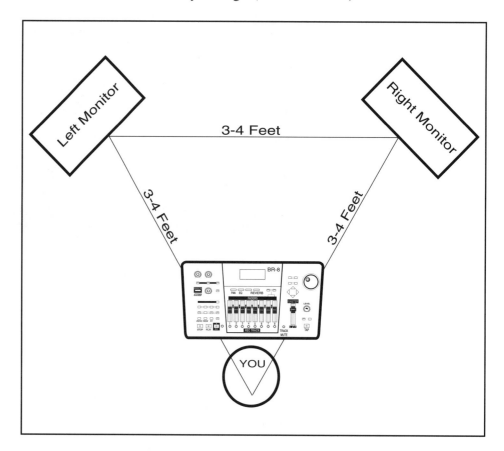

Vertical or horizontal

It all depends on the speaker, the manufacturer's suggestions, and how you hear. Below are illustrations of Alesis Monitor One's, a very popular and well thought of nearfield monitor. We use these in our studio, and at one time or another have placed the speakers in both positions using speaker stands. The bottom set up is the one Alesis suggests. However, I've had engineers come over, see that set up, and changed them to the top position. In fact, until they were repositioned, one engineer was so emotionally unsettled, he couldn't concentrate! The correct answer to positioning is that which gives the best sound in the room you're mixing and recording in.

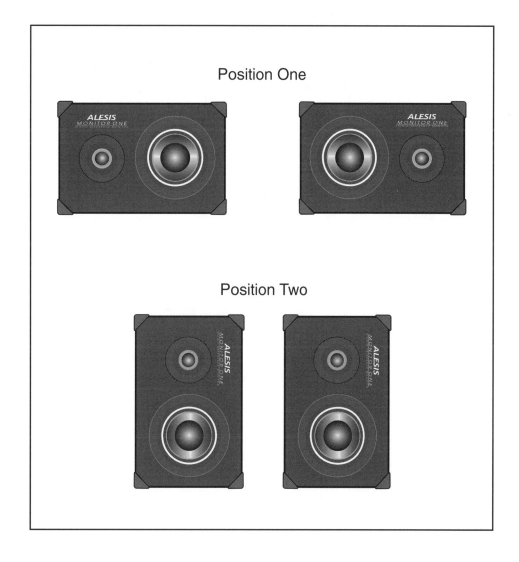

About speaker cable

People write dissertations on speaker cable. You're getting two paragraphs! You want true authentic speaker wire, not guitar cable. You can find it at music stores and Radio Shack. You want a heavy duty, medium gage wire. For most situations you'll want a No. 18 wire (up to 25' long). For 25' to 50' get No. 16, and No. 14 for 50' to 100'.

Rule of thumb: When the wire number is smaller, the speaker cable is thicker. When the wire number is higher, the speaker cable is thinner.

What's next

You now know how to connect speakers to the power amp and how to connect the amp to the mixing board. Setting up loudness levels comes later. Right now, our next step is learning how to connect effects to the aux sends and returns, and other goodies. As you learn this section, you'll learn the first steps of signal flow.

Connecting Aux Sends and Returns to the Mixing Board

This is a critical chapter because the concepts you learn here are directly applied to both smaller units and every digital audio program you're going to work with. The concept of Aux Sends and Returns is most often related to connecting outboard effects boxes to the mixing board. I'm breaking these into two categories: reverb and all other effects.

Very Simple - Outs and Ins

Where the struggle comes in working with the Aux Sends and Returns is understanding the basic definitions. A Send is an *out*. A Return is an *in*. Auxiliary means *alternate*. That's it. It's no more complicated than that.

Mono and Stereo

There are some effects boxes that are mono. Others are stereo. If it's mono, usually, there's *an* out and *an* in. If it's stereo, there are usually two outs and two ins.

Cable connections

Depending on the setup, most of the time you're using balanced cables. So it could be a 1/4" TRS to XLR, or 1/4" TRS to 1/4" TRS, or XLR to XLR.

Having said that, let's look at the connections on the Mackie board.

Mackie board connections

The 32-8 bus board allows for six Sends and Returns. Principle: hardware boards have a fixed number of Aux Sends and Returns. Virtual boards can have as many as the software is designed for. Remembering that data flows out to in, the AUX SEND (out) connects to the IN of the effects. The OUT of the effects connects to AUX RETURN (in of the board).

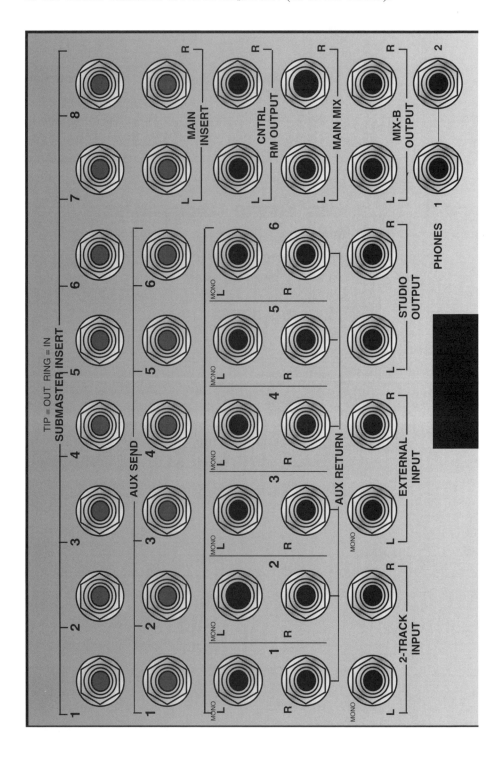

Connections with a Korg A3

The Korg A3 is an older effects unit from Korg USA. We use it in our studios and its got a beautiful sound. You can find them on e-bay. Additional effects can be found at www.korgaseries.org.

The front has a single input (as many effects units do). Here you can connect your electric guitar directly. The A3 is made up of effects chains which means that one program setting can blend reverb, compression, gates, exciters, etc. Units like this represent a great value because of their sheer versatility.

On the back panel, you see input, then output left and right.

1. Using a 1/4" TRS, connect Output Left on the A3 to Aux Return 1 on the board (see page opposite).

2. Using a 1/4" TRS, connect Output Right on the A3 to Aux Return 2 on the board (see page opposite).

3. Using a 1/4" TRS, connect Aux Send 1 from the board to the INPUT on the back of the A3. The unit is now connected.

Even though the Korg A3 is no more, this is how you connect these units. The connection scheme is consistent.

Like other effects units, the Korg A3 has MIDI connectors which lets its programs be called up by the sequencing program. To activate this feature, the effects unit has to be connected to a multiport MIDI device. Programs are changed using a patch command change.

Foot switches on the back let other aspects of the unit be controlled. Always consult your manual to find what's controlled here.

Audio signal flow

Now we're going to learn how to route the audio signal to the effects units and back.

We have to look in two places to start. First, on the channel strip look for Aux 1. It's the first knob below Trim. Turn it up to the mid position. On the page opposite, look for Aux Sends and Aux Returns. Notice the word, levels on both sides of the master panel. Flip back and look at the Korg A3 input connector. Above it there's a knob. Turn that knob (for this application) to the far right.

Lightly playing the instrument that's connected to the mixing board, begin working with the Aux Sends on the Master Panel to insure that the audio signal getting to the effects unit is hot enough. A light meter is normally on the effects unit. When the meter light goes into the red, it's indicating a hotter signal is going into the effects unit.

Now work both the Aux Returns and Aux Sends knob on the Master Panel to get the desired effects (which comes by experimentation only).

To review, here's what's happening, very simplified. There are two Aux Sends. One is on the channel strip the other is on the Master Panel. The Aux Sends setting on the *Master Panel* is the setting for the *whole board*. The Aux Sends setting on the *channel strip* is *just for that specific channel strip*. Once the Aux's on the Master Panel are set, the effects levels (also called the amount of Send) for *each* channel strip can now be adjusted. Since multiple effects boxes can be connected to the board, you can have multiple effects happening on individual channel strips. Again, how many depends on the board.

Understanding signal flow is a very critical concept.

Digital and virtual units use the concept of the aux send, without the hard cable connections. So until you understand this concept, your learning curve will be lengthened by all the options miniaturization and software offer you.

So let's review this one more time.

The audio signal from the channel strip is sent (*out* - Aux Sends) through the master Aux Sends to the effect unit. The effected sound is now sent back *into* the board (Aux Returns! - the *ins*).

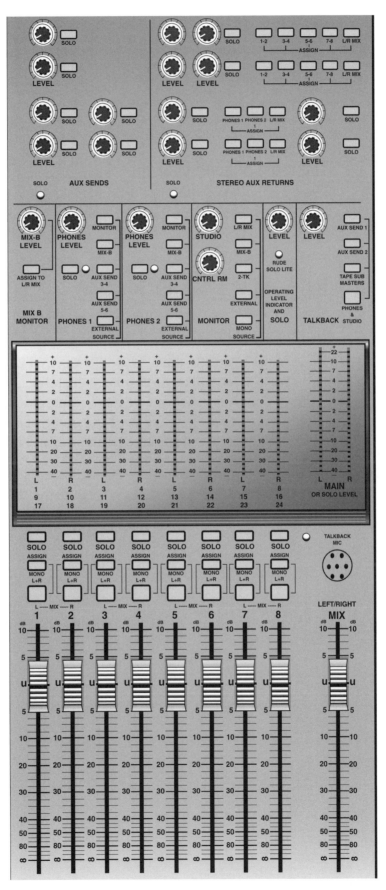

Thus, there are four levels to adjust:

1. the effects unit

2. the master Aux Sends

3. the master Aux Returns

4. the channel strip Aux Sends

The most difficult concept

Signal flow is one of the most difficult concepts to master, largely because of the technical language involved. There are no canned settings, you have to work with it.

Role of the Channel Inserts

The effects that go into the Aux Sends are the ones to be shared or applied to the most number of channel strips.

The channel inserts, to use a football term, are like special teams. They're special use effects like distortion, compression, gate, flanger, chorus, applied to one or two (stereo) channel strips. Now, this is a good generalization to get you going. As your experience grows, this generalization changes because you learn how to experiment and try new things to get unique results.

Connections to the Tascam

Having looked at the big Mackie 32-8 bus board, we now want to scope down to the Tascam unit. Here we want to look at the connections on the back of the system and gain an insight about signal flow, which we'll apply from the last few chapters. Here's a simple principle: connections reveal signal flow. So if you understand the connections (along with the connectors/cables needed to do the job), you can more quickly understand how to operate the board, or in the case of compact units like the Tascam, Korg and Roland pieces, the board/recorder.

Connecting to the back panel

Let's start with the most obvious, the XLR connectors. These are the four female XLR connectors with mic preamps. So this means that one end of the cable must be a male XLR and other end can be either an XLR connector or a 1/4" (either TS or TRS). This means that a mic can connect to these locations.

Above the MIC/LINE Inputs, you see 10 1/4" connectors. Inputs 1-6 are MIC/LINE Inputs. This means that a mic can be connected to this location. Since we've already learned that mics have XLR connectors, you'll need an XLR to 1/4" TRS cable to connect a mic to these connectors. If connected in mono, two or more MIDI keyboards can be connected to the MIC/LINE inputs.

Inputs 7-8 are the Stereo inputs where the outboard effects unit is connected. Outputs 9-10 are the Effect Sends 1 and 2. If you're using two mono effects like the A3, you can connect two outboard effects here. If you're using a stereo outboard effects box, you can connect one. Depending on the effects unit, these will most likely be 1/4" TRS cables.

Notice that the Monitor Outputs, the Line Outputs, and the Tape Outputs are all RCAs. So for the Monitor Outputs, your connections could be an RCA to RCA, RCA to 1/4" TS, or RCA to XLR unbalanced.

The monitor outputs can connect directly to either a boombox, a consumer power amp and speaker setup, or using the Hosa RCA to XLR cables, you could connect the Tascam to a professional power amp and pair of Alesis Monitor Ones.

The RCA line outputs let you connect to a tape deck. Depending on the professional quality of the tape deck, it might have either RCA connectors or 1/4" connectors. So that connection depends on the tape unit you're connecting to.

What I've covered represents the most basic audio connections for the Tascam. As you can see, there are a lot of similarities between the larger analog board and this smaller unit.

The mixing board area

Study the diagram on the opposite page.

Look immediately above the faders and you'll see the Effects Sends. If you'll study the controls, you'll see the effects choices. The teaching point is that what you're seeing is a greatly reduced version of the larger mixing board. And even though it's reduced, the visual concepts and the hard connections are still in place. The connection scheme and signal flow is obviously much simpler.

Unlike the Mackie board, this is a combination console and recorder. It's portable, and you're going to record and most likely mix in the same room you'd record in.

MIDI Syncing Note

At the sub input position on the Tascam, you can connect a MIDI tape synchronizer box which connects to a MIDI sequencer to sync up MIDI and audio.

Next up

With these concepts in mind, let's look at the connections for the Roland VS1880.

Connections to the Roland VS-1880

When we look at the Roland VS-1880, or the Roland BR-8, or the Korg D-Series units, a major change now occurs in our approach to recording. Digital units, thanks to miniaturization, can pack a lot of cool stuff in a very small area. The concept of how these digital board/recorders work, borrows directly from what you've just learned with the big analog board, scoped down to the smaller analog board/recorder. To understand the operations and signal flow of the digital recorder, requires that you understand the connections and the signal flow considerations we've just looked at. That's because miniaturization has done two things.

1. Miniaturization has altered the design and layout of the mixing board/recorder. There were clear design and layout similarities between the Tascam and Mackie units. Consistent design and layout create consistent and transferable work procedures. That's not the case with a digital unit. Here, there are no consistent design and layout features to help guide the work procedures. Both pro and home hobbyist must start at the very beginning. The pro can learn it quicker because he understands signal flow and board setup, and with a little help, can establish new work procedures in about a week or so. If you're not a recording pro, and your recording experience is minimal, then by default, you're going to have a longer learning curve because you're having to learn both recording signal flow concept and operations.

2. Miniaturization has allowed for the effects to be built into the unit directly or by acquiring expansion boards. So, there are no connectors for aux sends and returns. That's now a software function.

The VS-1880 back panel

You saw this diagram earlier where you worked out the cables that could be connected to the VS-1880. You can connect mics, keyboards, and amps to the 1880, but notice that there are no connections for external effects units to connect. This means that there are no hard connected aux sends and aux returns on this unit. To confirm that, turn the next page and look at the top panel of the VS-1880 and look for any labeling for aux sends, aux returns, effects sends, etc.

Recording external effects

External effects can be recorded when they're part of a chain. For example, if either an electric guitar or mic were connected to an effects unit, which was then connected to one of the mic/line inputs, the digital recorder would record the total sound with the effects.

The top panel

A quick glance at the top panel shows three recognizable features. These are the channel faders, the recording transport and the phrase Phantom Power, indicating that condenser mics can be connected to and powered by the VS-1880.

Learning steps for a digital unit

1. Locate the basic audio connections and determine the exact cables required to do the job.

2. Locate the parts of the channel strip (fader, mute, solo, pan, EQ, aux sends), some of which may be part of the software, and the button pushing routine for how to get there and use them.

3. Locate the signal flow for effects on an aux send and how it's applied to a specific channel strip and the button pushing routine for how to get there and use them.

4. Locate the signal flow for effects on channel inserts and how to create effects chains and the button pushing routine for how to get there and use them.

5. Determine the steps for arming the track and recording.

No criticism implied

The observations on design and layout I've made in this chapter are not a criticism on Roland, Korg or any company making hardware digital board/recorders. Make no mistake. These are phenomenal units that are jam packed with outstanding features and benefits. Yes, they do have longer learning curves. But the quality is so high, you can use them for years. So whatever time you put into them is worth it because the ROI on your time is longevity of use. And with high quality built into these units, who can complain about that!

The Computer, the Audio Card, the Mixing Board & More...

This chapter covers one of the most vexing problems I've seen with students: understanding the relationship of the computer and audio card to the mixing board and how to define your real system specs. What typically happens is that a student gets his board, then the computer and audio card, only to find out that he has a serious mismatch and the two aren't cooperating together.

For its TrueSpec line of systems, Alexander University clearly instructs both students and would be music computer purchasers to follow this pre-purchasing procedure:

1. define the software to be used and the audio drivers it implements.

2. define the audio card to be used.

3. define the mixing board to be used.

4. now define the remaining computer specs.

Much of this information is covered in my book, *How MIDI Works* 6th E.d. However, I want to give enough of a review here so that you understand how to approach this critical buying decision.

Defining specs: a quick review

Follow these simple steps.

Defining the software to be used and audio drivers

This is the first step. First define the software to be used based on the kind of music you're producing and recording. With this, it's critical that you find out ahead of time, which audio drivers the program can use, and which driver is the most stable.

- Cakewalk - MME, WDM

- Cubase - ASIO 2

- Emagic -EASI, ASIO 2

- Samplitude - MME

For Emagic, our experience today is that the ASIO 2 driver is well implemented and the one to choose since only three companies outside Emagic support the EASI driver standard.

Define the audio card to be used

At this writing for our TrueSpec line, we're mostly recommending the use of digital cards with the ADAT digital outs, specifically the RME Hammerfall Digi 9652 cards. That's because the drivers are rock solid for all the programs listed above including those running under Windows 2000. They sound fabulous. They're value priced because with the three ADAT Ins and Outs on the card, you can expand your system from 8 up to 24 audio ins and outs without ever changing your computer system. You simply increase the number of audio outs available by adding AD/DA converters. For price and value, the Alesis AI3 is a great unit.

Below is an all digital studio using the RME cards and the AI3.

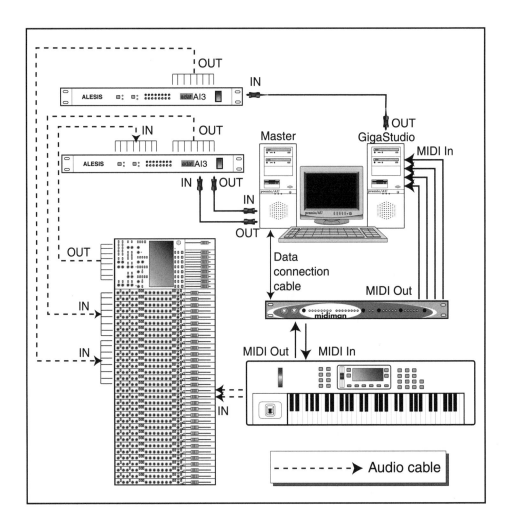

Here below is the system expanded. The expansion is coming from the second computer which is the GigaStudio system. GigaStudio permits up to 32 audio outs. The one RME card allows for 24. So the expansion comes from the addition of these AD/DA converters (the Alesis AI3).

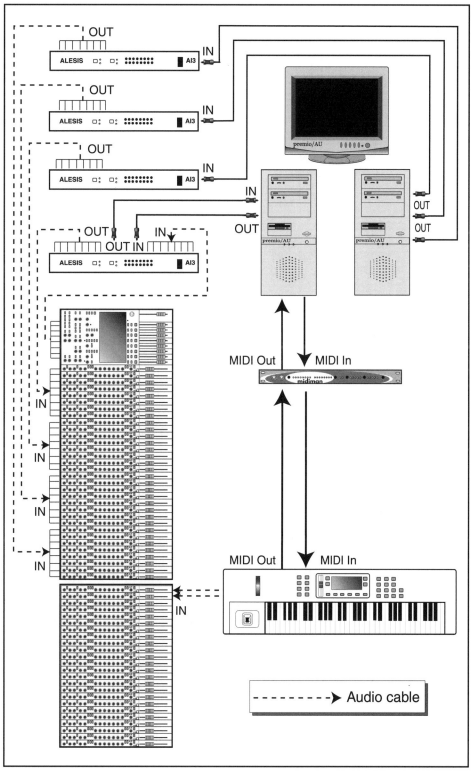

It may be that you neither want nor need such flexibility for expansion. In that case, an analog audio system built around the MIDIMan M-Audio line is the strongest choice as their audio drivers and sonic quality are excellent.

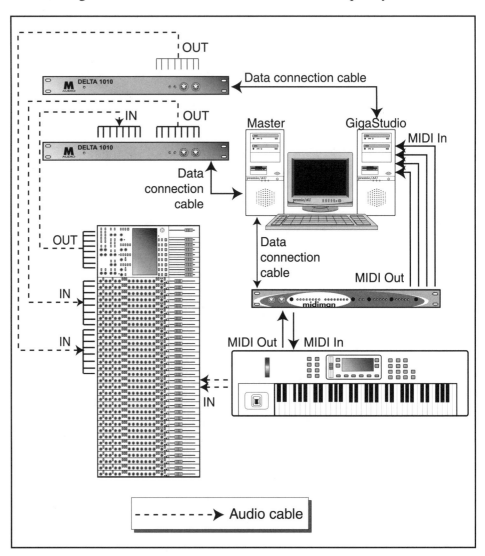

Define the mixing board to be used

This is the skipped step. There needs to be a match between the audio card and if you're going to seriously use virtual instruments, you need a true multiclient card with lots of audio outs. You also need a very flexible mixing board with a minimum of four bus master outs, eight is preferred. This is one of the reasons we favor the Mackie 8-bus board series. That's because the better audio cards have between 4 and 8 audio outs and ins. With a smaller board, the money you now invested in creating a powerful music computer has been diminished because the key component that it needs, a quality mixing board, is missing.

Now define the remaining computer specs

At very minimum, you realistically need a PIII - 600MHz with 256MB of RAM. However, I'm making these statements:

1. while the industry is in transition between the PIII and the P4.

2. while the PIII is operating with the newer 815 chipset permitting faster drives, but limiting RAM to 512MB.

3. while most of us are still using Windows 98SE because it works best for both audio and MIDI.

4. while we await the release of Windows XP which needs 128MB of RAM to load vs. 64 for Win98SE.

Which processor? Which DirectX?

When you look at the web sites of several companies making digital audio software, you'll need to note that the processor speed needs to be 400 to 450MHz or faster. Note that you don't find which processor they mean. Is it a PII? A PIII? A Celeron? An AMD? It can't be a P4 since P4s start at over a 1GHz speed. As of this writing, they're now up to 2.0 GHz and climbing!

If it's in the Pentium class, you can use on an existing machine a PII 450MHz, or a PIII 450MHz. But for anything above 450MHz you're now using PIIIs

So the question for the manufacturer is, if the recommended processor speed is 450MHz, is this saying that the software is not written to take advantage of the SSE instruction set for the PIII? I call this an unspoken issue because it's not really clear what system specs you need for optimum performance with the software. If the software is written for the SSE instruction set, you can get better performance, more stability and more audio tracks. If you migrate it to the P4, things get better. And when the software is upgraded to take advantage of the SSE-2, the P4 instruction set, things get even better from there.

How do you know if the software is optimized for either instruction set? By calling and asking, because no one is volunteering answers except for Samplitude 6.0, where they openly state it takes advantage of the Pentium 4 processor.

The next issue is DirectX implementation. At this writing we're up to DirectX 8a. You have to determine:

- which level of DirectX do the audio and video cards support
- which level of DirectX the host software supports
- which level of DirectX the external plug-ins support.

These issues are rarely discussed. But they all affect the audio and video card you purchase, which drivers are to be used, how well it interfaces with the software, and can directly affect audio performance by creating pops and clicks in your audio file.

Connecting the computer to the mixing board

There are two considerations:

■ analog to mixing board

■ ADAT optical to mixing board (analog or digital)

Analog to mixing board

I'll explain this concept using a MIDIMan Delta 1010 card connecting to a Mackie 32-8 bus board.

The Delta 1010 has two main parts: the PCI card that inserts inside the computer and the breakout box allowing for 8 audio ins, 8 audio outs and S/PDIF in and out. Below is the face plate for the Delta 1010. Notice that on the front panel, there are a pair of MIDI jacks for In and Out.

On the back of the 1010 are the jacks for connecting to the PCI card inside the computer, the audio inputs, the audio outputs, S/PDIF, and word clock.

■ The audio outs on the Delta go to the audio ins of the mixing board.

■ The audio outs on the mixing board go to the audio ins of the 1010.

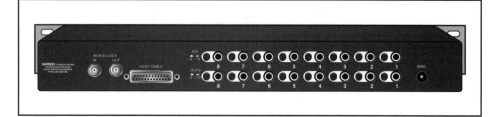

Mixing board connections

But which audio ins on the mixing board? And which audio outs on the mixing board?

Audio ins

The audio outs from the 1010 connect to the channel strips at the MIC/LINE connection (see below). Coming into the channel strips lets you hear the audio playback, and optionally apply EQ or other outboard effects so that the final mix is recorded to a DAT, a cassette, an 8-track DA88 tape, an ADAT Super VHS tape, etc. This means that you don't have to do the final work and mixing inside the computer. You can do it at the mixing board. It's your choice. Notice these use a 1/4" TRS to 1/4" TRS, or coming from the Delta, a 1/4" TRS to male XLR.

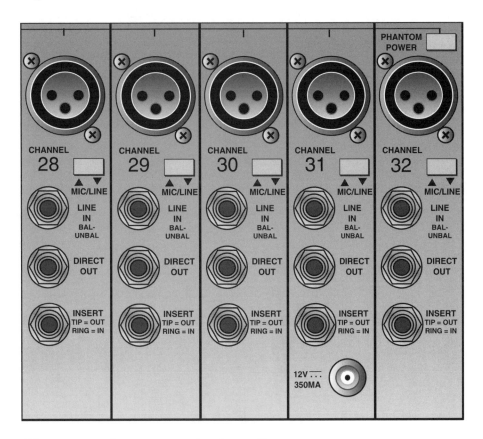

Please go to the next page for the audio outs.

Audio outs

We now have to run the audio from the mixing board to the Delta 1010. So let's think about this. The Delta 1010 has 8 analog ins and outs. The outs coming from the mixing board bring the audio signals that are going to be recorded as audio tracks into the Delta 1010 and into the computer. So what audio outs on the Mackie board do we use?

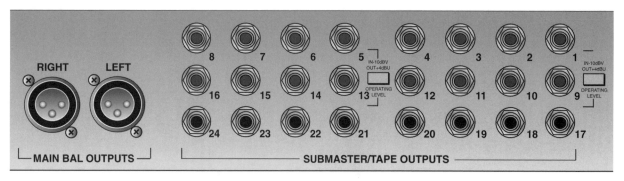

Look to the left and you'll see jacks labeled 1 through 8. These are called the submaster tape outs. These outs connect to the audio ins of the Delta 1010.

See the diagram below to see how the connections look.

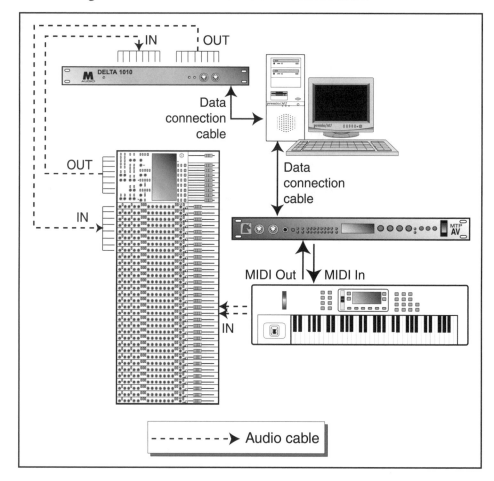

ADAT Connections

With one variation, the connections are exactly the same. The ADAT light-pipe card, in this case the RME-Hammerfall Digi 9652, connects into a PCI slot on the computer.

Instead of having a special cable that connects to a breakout box, the light-pipe cards use the TOSLink cables to connect to an AD/DA converter. Once that connection is made, the audio outs and ins to and from the mixing board are made exactly the same way. Below is the RME ADI-8 Pro, one of the best AD/DA converters in the world.

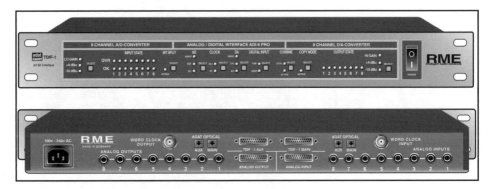

Connecting to an analog audio card without a mixing board

We're forever getting this question. There are some who want to bypass the mixing board and connect electric guitars, mics and so on, directly to the card to record directly into the computer. While this can be done, it's not advised as the audio cards need to have the audio signal coming in, at what's called *line level*. As we learned earlier, to bring an instrument up to line level requires the use of a mic preamp or a direct box.

One example of a mic preamp/direct box is the Omni I/O from MIDIMan (not pictured), which can be used as the front end of a Delta 66 or Delta 44 audio card. The Omni I/O will handle all of your signal flow from track laying to mixdown. It has a "split console" design, which means that the recording and monitoring sections function independently of one another. It uses both 1/4" and XLR inputs with phantom power, and features Effects Inserts as well as Send and Return connectors for you to add an external effects unit.

Here are some other examples...

Hosa DIB-307 Active DI Box

Another example is Hosa's Active Direct Box, the DIB-307, which you can use to boost guitar and bass signals up to line level to send direct to a mixing board. The DIB-307 has both 1/4" and XLR inputs and outputs plus a neat "Amp In" feature that lets you take the amplified signal from a guitar or bass amp, complete with any distortion or overdrive settings, and route it direct to the mixing board.

ART TUBE MP Studio

The TUBE MP Studio can be used as both a mic preamp and a direct box to connect guitars, synths and microphones to a mixing board. It uses 1/4" and XLR inputs and outputs and its sound is big, warm, and full.

JOEMEEK VC3Q Pro Channel

Some mic preamps come with added processing power built in and the VC3Q by JOE MEEK is one of them. This mic preamp features a compressor and EQ to help you shape your sound. Like the other units, it has 1/4" and XLR inputs and outputs.

Next Steps

The next chapter ties a lot of this together as we summarize signal flow on the analog board, then from the computer sequencer to the analog board.

Summary Basics of Signal Flow for the Analog Mixing Board

This section will consolidate in one place everything we've learned about the basics of signal flow on an analog mixing board. Then, how that knowledge is applied to understand the signal flow of software programs like Cubase and Logic. So let's take a quick review of what we've learned so far.

Organization of an analog board

The Mackie analog mixing board is organized into five broad sections:

- channel input/output
- master I/O
- channel strips
- master section
- back panel

Channel input/output

Here's where mics, lines from synths and guitars, and selected outboard gear are connected into the mixing board.

Mics

Mics connect to either the XLR jack or to where it's labeled LINE IN. Either way, you press the Mic/Line button so that it's in the UP position. This switches the circuitry so that the mic pre-amp (which boosts the audio signal coming into the board) is engaged. If the mic needs to be powered, called Phantom Power, it must be connected into the appropriate mic input(s) that have Phantom Power built in.

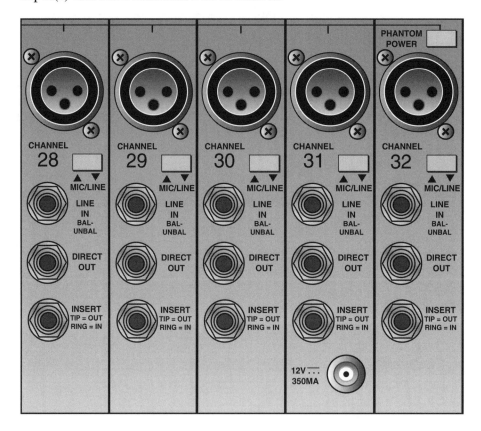

Synths and samplers

A synth or sampler is connected in the same jacks as the mic. It can either use the XLR connection or the 1/4" connection. The button is re-pushed so that pre-amp is disengaged. This area takes both 1/4" and XLR cables. Here the Mic Line button is pressed DOWN.

Direct Out

The Direct Out is where the audio can be connected to either an audio card or recorder. Staying with our RME example, 8 cables could be connected from the 8-bus outs to an AD/DA converter then to the RME card. Since the RME has 16 extra inputs, 16 channel strips could run directly into two more AD/DA converters, and then into the RME card. Result, 24 digital audio channels recording at once.

Insert

This is where a specific effect from an outside box or effects chain is inserted for that particular channel strip. Let's say you have an electric guitar coming into the channel strip. At the Insert, you can insert a distorted effect and it will only operate on that channel. If you want more than one effect by which to shape the electric guitar, you can daisy chain the different effects boxes for just that strip

Note!

The virtual mixing board inside any sequencing/digital audio program has no such connections. Any direct audio connections made are optionally made to the breakout box inputs when an analog audio card is used inside the computer. If the computer is using an RME-Hammerfall Digi 9652 with ADAT TOSLink connections, or other comparable card, then audio connections must either be made through a mixing board or directly into the external AD/DA converter, and here, it's more than likely that a Mic Pre-amp, or a direct box, may be needed to boost the audio signal to a recordable level.

Master I/O section

This is the section that enables you to hear your music through a sound system. Headphones and speakers are connected directly to the mixing board here. Also connected are the effects units used in the Aux Sends, 2-track inputs, and other effect inserts.

Note!

The virtual mixing board inside any sequencing/digital audio program has no such hardware connections. The audio from the audio card must be connected into an external sound source for music to be heard.

Please see illustration on next page.

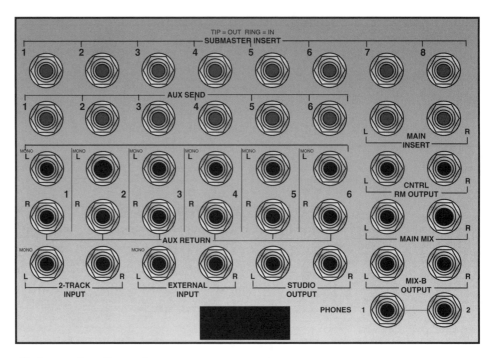

Submaster Inserts

This is an 8-bus board so there are 8 inserts. This is where a specific effect from an outside box or effects chain is inserted for that particular bus. Let's say you have a vocal coming into the channel strip. At the Insert, you can insert a compressor and it will only operate on that bus. If you want more than one effect by which to shape the vocal (or any audio assigned to that bus), you can daisy chain the different effects boxes for just that bus.

Main Mix

The audio signal goes out from this jack into either powered monitors or a power amp with speakers, or with live sound, to a PA system. Or you can run it directly to a DAT.

Control Room Output

Can also go to a power amp and monitors or powered monitor.

Main Inserts

As previously described, an effect can be placed here. It effects the audio signal from the main outs.

Headphones

There are two headphone jacks.

Two Track Input

This is where audio from a DAT or some other two track machine can be routed through the board.

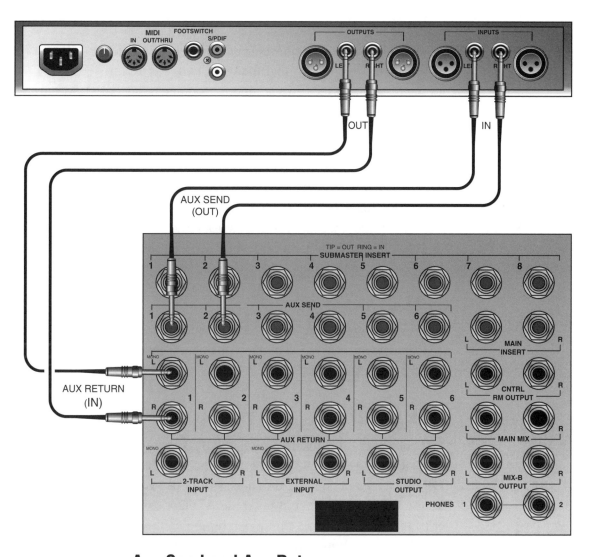

Aux Send and Aux Return

These two technical terms create a lot of confusion. To simplify, a *send* is an *out*, and a *return* is an in.

Aux Send - Most Common Use #1

Aux is short for *auxiliary* meaning *alternate* or *second*. So it's a second or an alternate send (*out*). The most common send (out) is sending the audio signal *out* from the board, to the *in* of a reverb unit. Look carefully at the illustration on the opposite page. The aux sends (out) from the Mackie board are going to the ins of this Lexicon MSX500.

Study the illustration above.

Aux Returns - Principle Use

The out of the reverb connects (you guessed it) to the Aux Return (in) of the Mackie board. Notice that there are two Aux Returns labeled L/Mono and Right. If the effect box is mono, it connects into the L/Mono jack. If it's stereo, it connects into both Left and Right Returns.

Study the illustration on the previous page.

The Golden Rule of Signal Flow and Audio Connections

Out to In. Just like with MIDI cable connections. That's because data flows out to in.

Aux Send - Second Use

This is most often used in live performance where the audio is going out from the board into, say, another set of monitors where the level is controlled by the Aux Send knobs.

Back panel

The back panel is critical to digital audio recording if you're using an audio card with more than two analog ins. On our Mackie 32-8 bus board, the TOP eight outs of the board connect to the 8 ins of either an analog card like the Delta 1010 or the 8 ins of an AD/DA converter. The AD/DA converter then connects to a digital Lightpipe card, or the 8 ins of the Alesis ADAT, allowing you to record up to 8 digital tracks of audio at a time.

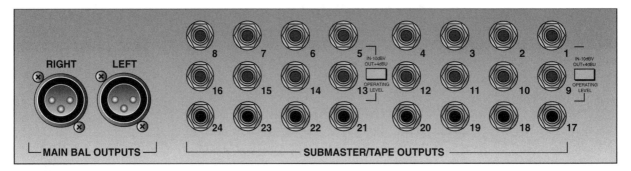

Note!

In the case of the RME Hammerfall Digi 9652 which permits 24 optical I/Os, using either three ADATs or three Alesis AI3 AD/DAs, you can record 24 outs directly into the computer for digital audio recording. However, the connections for that on an 8-bus board are different. Here, you connect direct from the channel strips into the card.

Key observation

If you're going to record digital audio tracks into your computer, then your analog mixing board needs to have at least two pairs of audio outs (one pair going to the speakers and one pair to the audio card in the computer). Depending on the kind of recording you're doing, the ability to record from 8 to 24 digital audio tracks can only be achieved with the correct mixing board.

Note!

Digital mixing boards often permit 24 I/O direct Lightpipe connections direct from the audio card. Here, the computer and the sequencing/digital audio program will either need three audio cards with Lightpipe connections (assuming the software program can handle it) or the one RME card. So, when looking for a digital mixing board, find out how many I/Os it can handle and whether or not you have to buy extra cards for the board to handle the extra inputs. This is a factor, for example, with the Roland VM-C7200 which can handle the 24 I/Os from the one card, but needs expansion cards from Roland to handle the extra 16 ins and outs.

Summary observations

Things that make sound, enhance sound, permit sound to be heard and recorded connect to the mixing board at the channel input, master I/O and back panel sections. The other two sections of the mixing board deal with manipulating the sound.

The channel strips

The channel strips are what enable you to mix and alter the sound coming in and out of the mixing board. Each channel strip contains:

- **volume fader** - which controls the level of the sound
- **solo** - which singles out one channel strip and mutes all others
- **mute** - which mutes one channel strip while allowing all others to be heard
- **pan** - which places the sound to the left, right, or center
- **bus assignments** (when the board has busses)
- **EQ section** - often a parametric EQ
- **aux ins** - which adjusts the effects levels
- **trim (also called gain)** - which boosts the audio signal of a line input

Channel strips

Trim or Gain

This is a second volume (level) knob that lets you raise or lower (aka boost or cut) the level of the audio signal. Used with the fader on the channel strip to set Unity Gain (0 dB).

Aux

Use this knob to control the level of effects coming (returning) to this channel strip. On the Mackie 32-8 bus board, there are four aux sends.

EQ

This is a parametric EQ. When doing digital recording, you have the option of EQ'ing at the board and then recording into the computer or hard disk recorder.

Mix B

This is the Mix B section of the Mackie board.

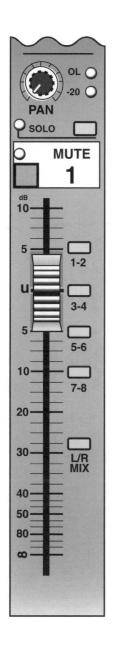

The fader section

This section controls the level (volume), panning, mute, solo and bus assignments.

Pan

Pan is short for panorama. This is where the audio is placed in the stereo spectrum.

Solo

Press this button to single out the audio signal assigned to that channel strip from the rest of the mix.

Mute

When pressed, turns off or removes the audio from a specific channel strip from the mix.

Channel Fader

This is the slider that controls the volume level for that channel strip. The U to the left is Unity Gain or 0dB.

Bus Buttons

When pressed, the audio from this channel strip is sent to one of the 8 buses on this board. Using a synth concept, you can create a giant "layer" (like all the strings) and bus them down to a specific bus fader. Now the single bus fader controls the level (volume) of all the strings assigned to it. L/R Mix is the master fader.

Why you have to understand channel strips

Below is a drawing of the Roland BR-8. As we discussed in an earlier chapter, notice it has no channel strips, as you just observed on the Mackie board. So in digital units like this where controls have been miniaturized or turned into software features, the channel strip has to be "built" (e.g., discovered, found, located, *built!*).

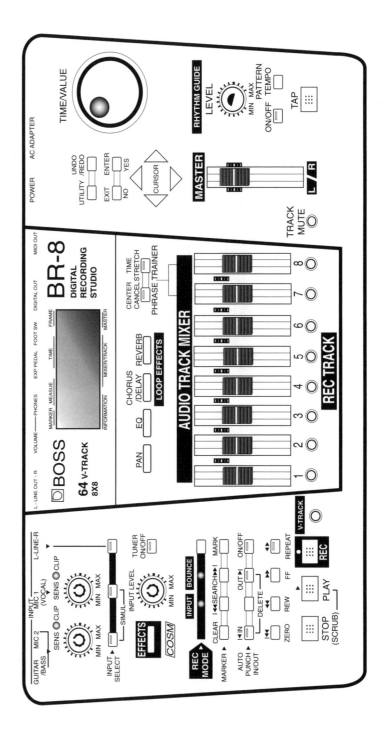

Channel strips in Cubase 32 5.0

Here's a screen shot of Cubase 32 5.0 for one audio track. Notice that the channel strip, instead of being vertical, is like a panel. Below you see the fader, the solo and mute buttons. Less obvious is the pan which is the thin line immediately below Solo. To the right of the fader are the effects inserts, then the "Sends." Cubase 32 5.0 has 8 sends. By comparison the Mackie board has 6. Next to the "Sends" is the EQ section. So in Cubase, the left to right reading of the channel strip doesn't follow the layout of an analog board channel strip. If it did, the order would be fader area, EQ, sends, *then* inserts.

Insert Effects

If I click a button labeled DYN, we get this configuration which hides the EQ, but brings up two effects, the Gate and Compressor, which normally would be used in the Channel insert section of the mixing board. Here, the software has it in place for each channel strip.

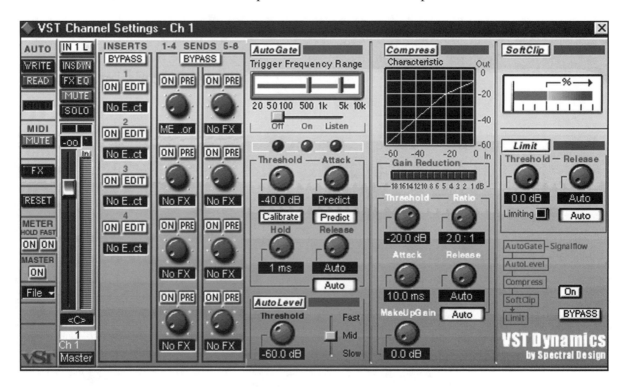

Channel strips in Logic 4.61

Here's a screen shot of a group of faders in Emagic Logic's virtual mixing board. This is a very "Mackie-like" design. Compared to Cubase, notice that this is a vertical channel strip. Also notice that the order of the channel strip, like Cubase, is also different. While the fader, mute, solo and pan features are in predictable locations, the position of the EQ (which I activated on one channel strip), sends, buses and inserts are in the same order as Cubase, but not like the Mackie board. One EQ advantage of this board is that if you use the preset (see fader #1), on each fader, you can see all the EQs in a single glance, like you would an analog board.

In a virtual mixing board, however, EQ can be inserted on individual channel strips in the Insert section. When you do that in Logic, you lose the visual sweep. So to see the EQ settings, you have to open each inserted EQ.

In this shot I opened the EQ added as an insert in the channel strip. You can do this in Cakewalk, Cubase and Emagic. When you've finished EQ'ing that track you close the EQ window.

Inserting EQs from other companies

You can also get third party EQs. Below, is the "Q" from TC Electronics Native Essentials package. This is a professional level EQ used for both recording and mastering. Here I inserted it in Logic, but I could have inserted it in any of the programs.

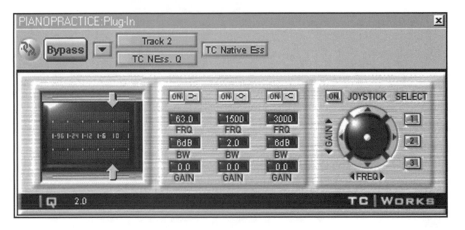

Channel strips in Samplitude 2496

Samplitude 2496 operates on a completely different concept. With Samplitude, you can edit and mix at the track level, or with the individual audio file within the track. The audio file within the track is called an *object*. Below, on the upper left, you'll see the software channel strip for muting, (M2), soloing (S), lock track (L), volume (V) and panning (P). (R) is for recording. The volume slider and the pan slider work like conventional faders. However, when (V) or (P) are selected you can draw in volume and panning data.

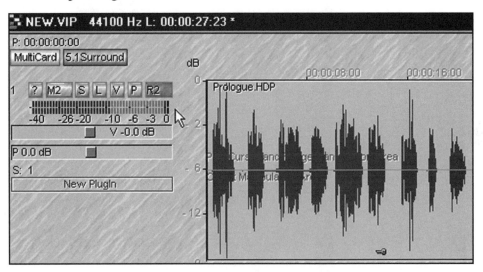

In this screen shot, I've highlighted the audio object in the track that I want to mix/edit.

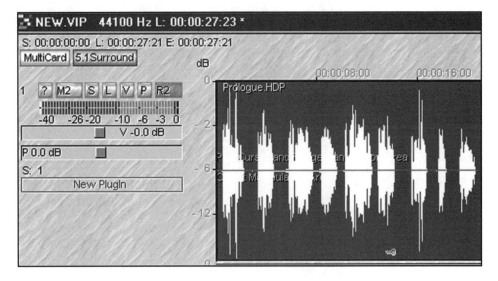

On the next page, look at the Effects menu on the far right. All of these options are available for just that one object.

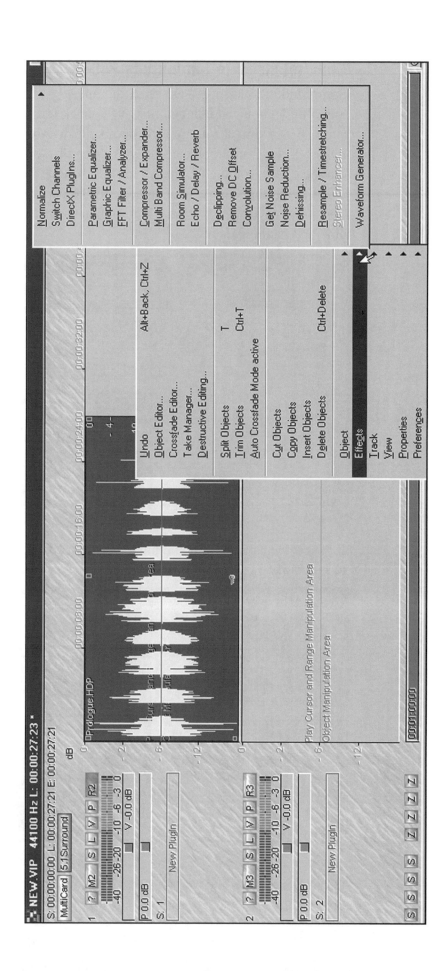

On this next screen shot, instead of selecting the Effects menu I selected the object edit menu. Observe that the object edit menu is also a channel strip, but for that object. You have a compressor, parametric EQ, volume and pan.

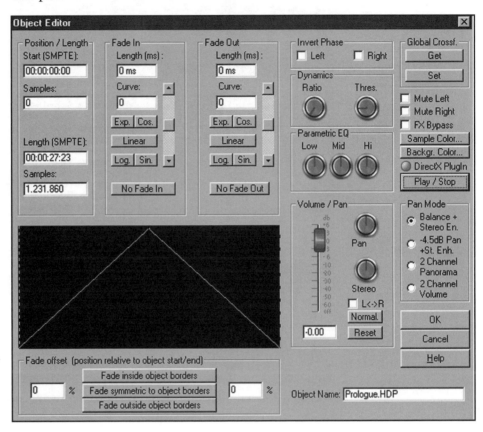

Across from the parametric EQ is the button to insert DirectX Plug-ins. It doesn't say Insert but that's what it is. So when you click on that Insert button, you get this:

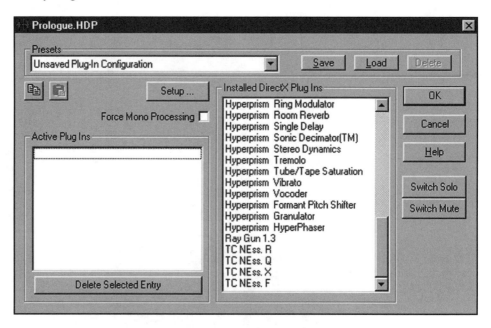

What all this means

Understanding the parts of the channel strip and how they work is the secret to speed learning digital audio software programs and hardware units.

Critical procedural learning step

Part of the procedural operations of any hardware or virtual digital mixer is to first locate the parts that make up the channel strip. Simply put, you have to find where everything is. Until you've done that, you're operationally lost.

Golden Rule of engineering and mixing

If you can run one channel strip, you can run the mixing board. But with digital and virtual mixing boards, first you have to *find* the channel strip.

Understanding busing

Let's say that on your analog board you have 4 channel strips dedicated to just violins (very common in MIDI recording). Each fader is set to a different volume level that's created the composite blend that you're now happy with. To make a group volume correction, you press one of the bus buttons to the right of the fader. For this example we'll pretend you pressed 1-2 for all four channel strips. This sends the channel's audio signal down to bus fader 1-2. So that one bus fader now controls the volume of all four channels, without losing your blend.

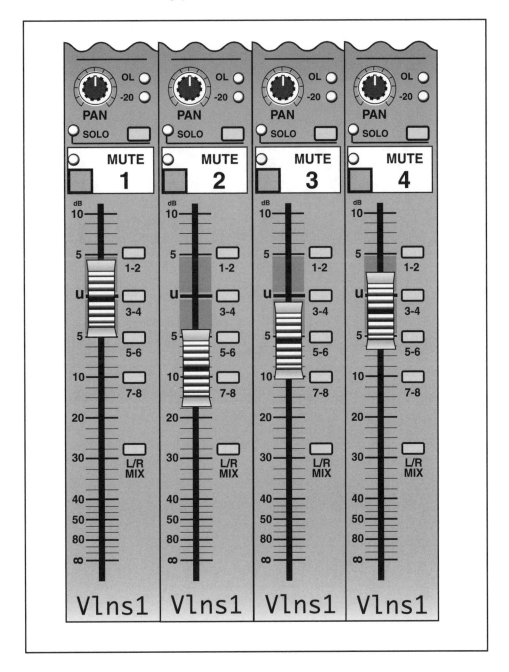

Busing lets you do this. On the Mackie 32-8 bus board, you have 8 buses. You can set up to have 8 mono faders or 4 stereo pairs. The choice depends on the recording assignment you're doing, the client needs, and the kind of equipment your work will be played back on as they create the final mix.

On the fader on the Mackie board, you press the appropriate bus button, here labeled 1-2, 3-4, 5-6, 7-8.

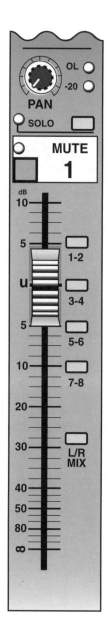

The sound is now bused to the appropriate fader in the master section which controls the volume level of all the channel strips assigned to it. If the signal is mono (like a voice, a solo instrument, etc), then on the Mackie board, for the odd numbered bus fader (1,3,5,7), you turn the Pan knob to the far left as far as it will go. This is called *hard left*. For the mono audio signal to go to the even number bus faders (2, 4, 6, 8), you turn the Pan knob to the far right, as far as it will go. This is called *hard right*.

See diagram on next page.

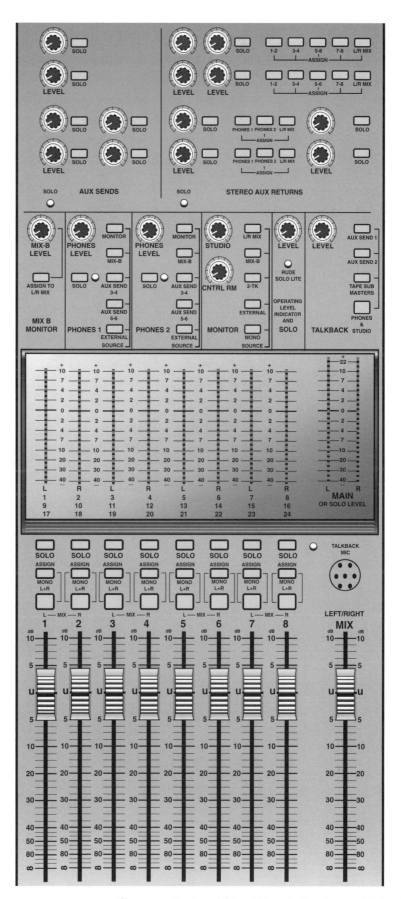

Changing volume levels during the recording

With an analog board, there are two ways to change the volume during the final mix. The first is to purchase an expensive automated mixing package to run the board. The second is manually, with your hand! In recording circles this is called *riding the faders*. However, in the next chapter, you're going to learn how to set up the board and control the volume (called an automated mix) directly from the sequencing/digital audio program.

In the newer digital audio boards, you get motorized faders.

Signal Flow Between the Mixing Board and the Sequencer

The systems are hooked up, and you now understand the fundamentals of how an analog mixing board works. Now comes the next step which is understanding the signal flow between the sequencer and the mixing board.

First issues

Before there can be signal flow, you must first assign:

1. Specific synths to specific tracks

2. Programs

3. Initial volume levels from which to start

Depending on how complex your piece of music is, this can take from a few minutes to a few hours.

Virtual instruments

Cakewalk, Cubase and Emagic now have an entire series of virtual instruments that run directly within the program. You must determine:

1. Where they are

2. How to insert them

3. How to change programs/samples

4. Save/store programs/samples

5. Set volume levels

6. Set panning

Note:

Since all of the major programs on the Mac and PC have virtual instruments, you must now determine where they are and where they figure into establishing Unity Gain levels. These plug-ins are usually inserted into the virtual audio mixing board but implemented in the arrange window.

Second issues

The second issues to deal with are:

1. Setting up the audio levels of all synths and samplers at the mixing board

2. Setting up pan and levels within the sequencer

3. Determining what will execute the audio levels of the synths and samplers for the mix:

   a. Controls within the sequencing program itself

   b. An external mixer like the Peavey PC1600x

   c. The mixing board itself, thus bypassing all virtual controls

4. Setting the audio levels for "live" performers like vocalists, guitarists, etc.

Setting up the audio levels of all synths and samplers at the analog mixing board

Here we deal with a concept called Unity Gain, or what engineers call zeroing out the board. The object is to get all modules and the selected programs sounding at the same volume level. Once that's been achieved you're now ready to start the pre-mix.

Starting procedures

1. If the synth or sampler is connected with both left and right outputs, set the pan position at the mixing board for the left fader all the way to the left (called hard left) and the pan position for the right fader at the mixing board all the way to the right (called hard right).

2. Set the faders at the U or 0 mark on the channel strip.

3. Push the volume fader on the synth or sampler up to full position. Keep it in that position.

4. Select the program or sample you want to use.

5. Now tap the keyboard lightly to firmly starting with one pitch only. Watch the meter bridge or light meters on the mixing board. They'll also be marked with a U or 0 or some other clear marking (sometimes a long dash) to show where Unity Gain is. Repeat with a two part chord, then a three part chord. Watch the meter bridge for where the sound hits with one, two and three pitches sounding. This sounds silly until you begin monitoring inside the software sequencer.

6. If the program in the synth is too hot, you go to the trim (also called gain) control (NOT the fader on the channel strip) and turn it slowly to the left until you've hit 0 (U).

7. If the program in the synth or sampler is too soft, you go to the trim (also called gain) control (NOT the fader on the channel strip) and turn it slowly to the right until you've hit 0 (U).

8. Repeat this procedure for all programs coming into the board assigned to specific faders.

The pre-mix without the PC 1600x

The pre-mix is actually where you start the mixing process before recording.

9. For the ensemble you're recording, once Unity Gain has been set, set the pan position so that the instrument's position in the speakers reflects its position in a live performance.

10. To start, we'll assume that within the sequencing program, one instrumental sound is assigned per track. You can now set the panning position for that sound ("instrument") inside the sequencer.

11. Once done, you must now decide which MIDI value in Volume will be Unity Gain! There are two typical numbers used: 90 and 100.

Quick test

12. Set the track volume for 90. Tap the master keyboard controller as before and see where the levels come up to on the meter bridge of the mixing board.

13. Reset the track volume for 100. Tap the master keyboard controller as before and see where the levels come up to on the meter bridge of the mixing board.

14. Chances are you'll discover that Unity Gain is at neither setting. Now you must make an arbitrary decision which number will reflect Unity Gain at the analog board. My preference is 90, because it gives you some "head room" in the MIDI spec (remember, MIDI is numbered from 1 to 127 or 0 to 128). Additionally, you have to be thinking dynamics. One number is going to reflect *fff (very, very loud)*. A second number will reflect *ff (very loud)*. A third number will reflect *f (loud)*. A fourth number will reflect *mf (moderately loud)*. A fifth number will reflect *mp (moderately quiet) and so on*. So once you've set 90 in the sequencer as your arbitrary Unity Gain, reset the trim (gain) on the analog board so that when you play the master keyboard controller for each program, you can see Unity Gain being reached on the mixing board.

What about 0 in Digital

Later, we'll discuss setting 0 inside the virtual digital mixer. Understand that 0 in analog and 0 in digital have two different meanings. In analog, you have "headroom", which means that if you go over 0 a little, it's no problem. But in digital, it's a major problem because there is *no* headroom, so if you go above 0 you get digital clipping, a nasty kind of distortion. So the signal being recorded inside the digital sequencer must be less than 0 by usually 3.5dB. This can be controlled by the virtual mixing board. In a board like the Mackie where you have 8 buses, you just back down the bus faders 3.5dB. This keeps the mixing board in the same position and the sequenced mix in the same position, but the incoming signal at a slightly lower level.

What executes the mix inside the sequencer

A realistic problem with mixing inside the sequencing/digital audio programs is getting an exact mix using the mouse with the faders. Factors for smooth movement include the mouse, the mouse ball (if it's clean!), the mouse pad (new or worn), your mouse settings inside Windows, how your studio is set up and the position of your hand to the mouse, and finally, how well the faders in the program respond to mouse moves with the human hand, which can be pretty jerky when using a mouse.

For serious recording, the best way around this is the use of an external MIDI mixing console. Our recommendation is the Peavey PC1600x because of price, quick installation, and the number of preset programs available to give you the recording control you need.

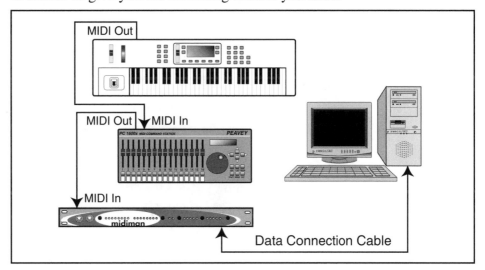

Once the MIDI data is recorded and edited, the next phase is working out the dynamics. To do this, using overdub recording either directly on the track or in the piano roll edit, you record your volume changes and use the fader from the PC 1600x for raising and lowering volumes. Within the sequencing program, you then edit and put in the final polish.

Executing at the mixing board

If you're executing a piece with few dynamic changes, it's faster to do the mix at the analog mixing board. Thus, once you've keyed in the sequence, you can make final quick adjustments at the board, then record either directly to tape or into the sequencing/digital audio program for the final two-track recording.

However, you do have other options available for automation. For example, if your mixing board is digital like the Roland VS1680, Yamaha O2R or O1V, you can purchase C-MEXX software that installs in the PC, and via MIDI, can control and automate the entire mix.

Pre-mixing

Once you have all your programs and samples picked with basic blends worked out, the next step is to more thoroughly work out the volume levels based on the "ensemble" you're writing for. This means you:

1. Re-check the ensemble's panning

2. Re-set the volume levels within the sequencing program for a more natural sound. For example, even though you may have the flute and the cello section at Unity Gain, their individual levels within the arrangement are going to be different. Thus the initial levels you set will be refined as you proceed with your piece and set the appropriate dynamics levels.

In this pre-mixing stage get as close to accurate as possible, as your musical thinking will be affected if you don't.

Sub-mixing within a synth or sampler

If you have a very large budget with an equally large mixing board (and possible side car) along with enough synths and samplers, you can have one program per audio out (mono) or one program for every stereo pair. For example, if I use 5 GigaStudios in my studio each with 32 audio outs and I could accommodate all 32 outs, I'd have to have a mixing board capable of handling 160 inputs! Obviously, this isn't very practical. So how do we set up the mixing board when we potentially have more audio outs than we do inputs on the board?

The answer is submixing. Here, the sampler or synth is treated as a mini-mixer with levels and panning set up within the unit and programs assigned to specific audio outs. Let's look at a simple example using the Emu E4.

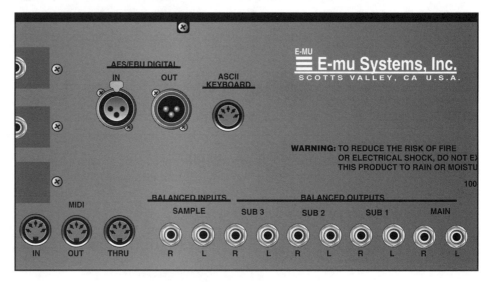

The Emu E4 has four pairs of audio outs: main, sub 1, sub 2 and sub 3. The E4 also contains an excellent effects unit (plus a sequencer for those who need it). From the factory, the E4, like all other units, has 16 MIDI channels.

Let's say for this project, I'm using the String Orchestra sample from the Kirk Hunter Strings (Ilio Entertainments), plus Violin Pizz and Bass pizz from the same library. Next, I have a French horn and trombone from Roland (the E4 also reads the Roland and Akai libraries), a tambourine and timbales (from the Emu library), and finally, flute and oboe from the Miroslav mini-disk. This should pretty much max out the E4! Now, with all those orchestral sounds, how do I set levels and panning within the E4?

First, you make sure all four stereo pairs are connected to the mixing board. Second, you assign the programs to be used by instrumental family to a specific audio out.

Main	Sub1	Sub2	Sub3
Strings	*FH*	*Tambourine*	*Flute*
Violins Pizz	*Bones*	*Timbales*	*Oboe*
Bass Pizz			

Each one of the E4 stereo pairs are assigned to a specific pair of faders on the mixing board.

1. Use the sequencing program to pan each program within the E4 where it would normally fall if it had its own fader.

2. Now set the individual volume levels to Unity Gain as you learned earlier in the chapter.

3. Now blend.

Notice that in these steps I did the panning first, then the levels. As you go along, you'll adjust the volume levels in the sequencer to avoid distortion.

What about GigaStudio?

Gigastudio gives even more options. For analog cards, like the Delta 1010, you can have 8 audio outs. If you use the Digi 9652 card and three Alesis AI3's, you get 24 audio outs. Same approach, just more audio outs.

Mixing below the track level

Both Cubase and Emagic let you sequence and make adjustments within the track for individual sequences. In Cubase this is called a Part. In Emagic, it's called a sequence, or it could be called an object.

Cubase

In Cubase, after you've done the main recording, the bulk of your editing is done in piano roll edit, which Cubase calls Key Edit. Here, you're mostly making dynamic changes to the individual Parts, rarely to the track as a whole. When using Ghost Tracks, as the main track updates, so do the Ghost Tracks.

Emagic Logic

In Emagic, you do most of your work on the main screen where you see the rhythm of the pitches you're working with. Your work is done within Hyper Draw for each individual sequence you record. Here, you're mostly making dynamic changes to the individual Aliases, rarely to the track as a whole. When using Aliases, as the main track updates so do the Aliases assigned to that track.

Other work is done with Hyper Edit for each respective sequence.

Working out the blends

There are times when two or more programs or samples are combined together to create a more complete instrumental sound. Here, the programs must be blended. But where? At the mixing board or inside the sequencing program? This depends on the approach and the program you use.

Cubase

For example, if you use the Bus/Master Fader approach with Ghost Tracks, or if you just copy the tracks to another, you have to set the blend level directly at the mixing board by raising or lowering the fader to create the blend. This way the sequencer is always at Unity Gain. If you want to keep the board at Unity Gain, then you have to re-record the crescendo/decrescendo for each track in the blend.

Emagic

If you use the Bus/Master Fader approach with Aliases, or if you just copy the tracks to another, you set the blend level internally with Emagic or if you're using the Peavey PC 1600x, directly with the synth or sampler. This way the mixing board is always at Unity Gain.

24 Signal Flow on the Virtual Mixing Board in Samplitude and Emagic

I've spent lots of time on connections and signal flow because it's the procedural heart of how you record. If you don't understand this concept and how it applies to virtual mixing boards, digital boards, digital board/recorders and analog boards, you can find yourself lost in a sea of button pushing routines. This is compounded by language changes from one company to another to describe the same button or concept.

So in this chapter I want to cover two virtual mixing boards, those from Samplitude and Emagic to show how these concepts work. While different, both mixing boards are similar in their implementation to a hardware mixing board, including the correct recording language.

Samplitude

Previously, we had a basic review of Samplitude. I now want to add in the mixer and the aux sends to complete our concept of signal flow.

Turning Busses on and off

Above the first channel strip in Samplitude 6.0 is the Busses button. When clicked, the Busses appear as a separate track. When unclicked, they don't appear at all.

The Samplitude virtual mixing board

Look at the top of the virtual mixing board and you'll see that I can have four (4) AUX SENDS. The area is labeled Aux Bus Sends (look to the left under Gain). Right now, the Aux Bus Sends are all off.

To activate the Busses, I right click on off. To the lower left in Samplitude, you'll see Track 5. and its labeled AUX 1. I then left click on the off button in the mixer and AUX 1 appears in the mixer. See the screen shot below.

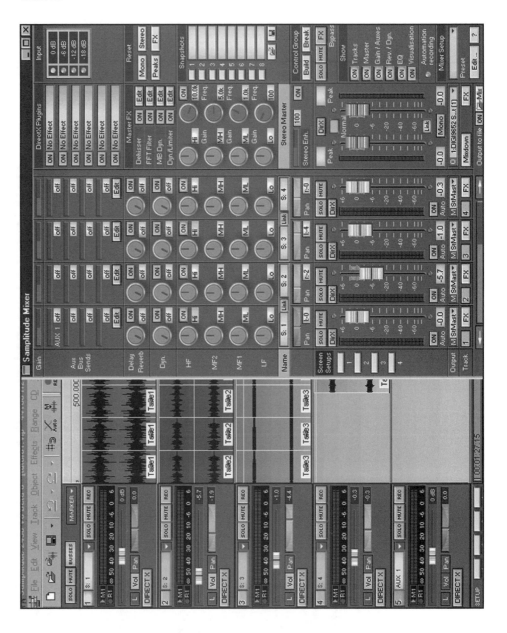

You now go to Track 5 in the mixer. Here you see the label, DIRECT X. You click once on the DIRECT X button to bring up the effects available to pick from.

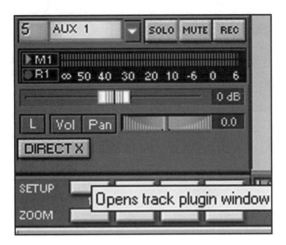

Here's your list. I highlighted TC Works Native Reverb.

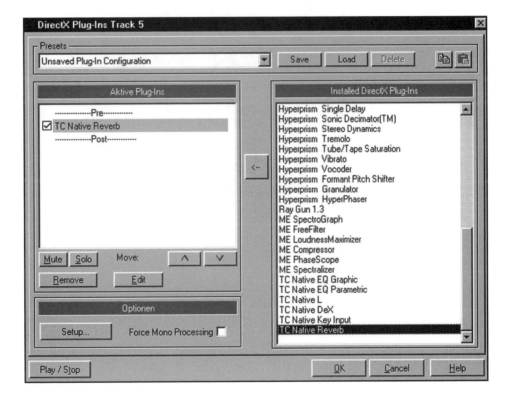

Now here's the selected effect.

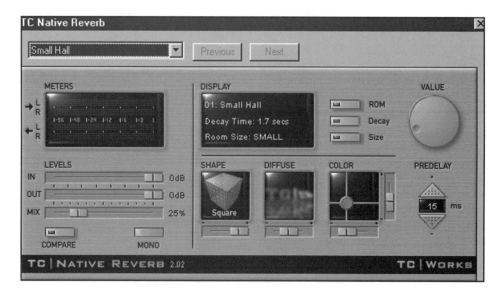

On the Samplitude virtual board, I now set the AUX 1 level. It's at 3.3.

Now on AUX 1 channel fader I set my levels just like I did on the Mackie board. Here it's set for 2.0. It's name shows up (TC Native Reverb) and I have an ON button to turn it on or off. The reverb is now implemented with the AUX SENDS.

Emagic Logic

Now let's set the Aux Sends with Logic. There are two terms to keep track of: Returns and Sends. First, look below at the Logic channel strip. You see Inserts, and directly below that, Sends.

On the Returns, you see several labels: Returns, Bus 1, Inserts. Under Inserts, I've set up an effect, TC Native Reverb, Large Bright Hall.

Now I go back to the channel strip and at Sends, I press and hold down the mouse button and get these choices. Since I put the TC Native Reverb on Bus 1, that's what I select here.

Now notice that I have a little dial and under Sends I see Bus 1. The little dial is the volume fader and controls the effects level for that fader. The Aux Sends are now set up. You repeat the process to add more aux sends and returns.

Microphone Basics

The subject of microphones and mic placement is a book and course in its own right. To give you everything you need to know in an entry level title is simply not possible. Thus, I've organized the instruction for you in three chapters. In this chapter, you'll learn the types of mics and mic patterns. In chapter 26, I touch on stereo miking. Chapter 27, The Shure Gallery of Microphone Positions, gives you one and two mic placement positions for grand piano, amps, acoustic guitar, drums, vocalist and choir. This covers common situations that can be applied with nearly any kind of recorder for singer/songwriters, rock bands, pianist/vocalist, etc.

Setting Expectations

There are certain things about mics that you can learn and memorize. But the real knowledge comes from trying and doing. Everything, and I mean everything, about mic selection and placement involves your ears. Your skill grows as you record. The results you get depend on the mic itself, where you're recording, the recorder, the medium you're recording on (digital tape vs. hard disk recorder vs. software program), and the performer.

In Chapter 27, you'll notice that all of the mic positions are set up with the Shure SM-57. The SM-57 is the world's most used mic. It's financially accessible to most with a street price of around $100.00 US. The SM-57 is a great mic, and a great place to start. If you want to learn two and three mic setups, a little saving and you've got two-three mics to do it with. As both your experience and confidence grow, you can advance and purchase different mics.

In his book, *The Recording Studio Handbook*, John M. Woram, who edited db Magazine, stated his law of correct microphone usage:

NEVER use more than two microphones.

Woram points out that if engineers really followed this rule, few sessions could take place, but its importance rests in understanding how to make one and two mics work for you before setting up additional ones.

Hence, why we've limited illustrations to one and two mics.

Mics and patterns

There are three basic types of mics:

- Condenser

- Dynamic

- Ribbon

There are five pickup patterns:

- Omnidirectional

- Cardioid (also unidirectional)

- Supercardioid (also unidirectional)

- Hypercardioid (also unidirectional)

- Bidirectional

Depending on its design, generally, any mic type can have any of the pickup patterns designed into it. Some mics have multiple pickup patterns. The only way to tell is to go to the factory web site, look up the mic you're thinking about and see the type it is and its pickup pattern(s).

Note:

For the balance of this chapter and the next, I've paraphrased liberally from "Shure's Microphone Techniques for Music Studio Recording."

The three mic types

To repeat, the three mic types are condenser, dynamic, and ribbon.

What mics are

Says Shure, "A microphone is an example of a 'transducer,' a device which changes energy from one form into another, in this case from acoustic into electrical." The type of transducer is defined by the operating principle. In the current era of recording, the two primary operating principles used in microphone design are the dynamic and the condenser.

Condenser

These are considered the most accurate mics and add the least amount of coloration to the sound. They're often chosen for acoustic instruments like guitar, piano, strings, vocals, brass, woodwinds and percussion. They're also used for recording the ambient sound of a room. Condensers capture a wide range of frequencies without having to be "right up on" the performer. However, the downside of this advantage is that in a live performance, feedback can be created. Condensers have to be powered. Most often this is done by turning on the Phantom Power feature of the mixing board. In other cases, the condenser may come with a battery.

A condenser microphone uses a conductive diaphragm and an electrically charged backplate to form a sound-sensitive "condenser" (capacitor). Sound waves move the diaphragm in an electric field to create the electrical signal. To use this signal from the element, all condensers have active electronic circuitry, either built into the microphone or in a separate pack.

This means that condenser microphones require Phantom Power or a battery to operate. However, the condenser design allows for smaller mic elements, higher sensitivity and is inherently capable of smooth response across a very wide frequency range.

The main limitations of a condenser microphone relate to its electronics. These circuits can handle a specified maximum signal level from the condenser element, so a condenser mic has a maximum sound level before its output starts to be distorted. Some condensers have switchable pads or attenuators between the element and the electronics to allow them to handle higher sound levels.

Distortion

If you hear distortion when using a condenser microphone close to a very loud sound source, first make sure that the mixer input itself is not being overloaded (if it is, then lower the trim.)

If not:

1. Switch in the attenuator in the mic (if equipped)
2. Move the mic farther away
3. Or use a mic that can handle a higher level

In any case, the microphone won't be damaged by excess level.

A second side effect of the condenser/electronics design is that it generates a certain amount of electrical noise (self-noise) which may be heard as "hiss" when recording very quiet sources at high gain settings. Higher quality condenser mics have very low self-noise, a desirable characteristic for this type.

Dynamic

Also called moving coil. These are the most durable of all mic types. The Shure SM57 is an example. They're best used close to the performer or instrument, usually within a distance of less than a foot.

Says Shure, "Dynamic microphone elements are made up of a diaphragm, voice coil, and magnet which form a sound-driven electrical generator. Sound waves move the diaphragm/voice coil in a magnetic field to generate the electrical equivalent of the acoustic sound wave. The signal from the dynamic element can be used directly, without the need for additional circuitry. This design is extremely rugged, has good sensitivity and can handle the loudest possible sound pressure levels without distortion. The dynamic has some limitations at extreme high and low frequencies. To compensate, small resonant chambers are often used to extend the frequency range of dynamic microphones."

Ribbon

Another type of dynamic mic, best used close to the subject. It's called a ribbon mic, because as described by John Woram, "a thin corrugated sheet or "ribbon" of metal foil takes the place of the diaphragm/moving coil combination." Modern ribbon mics, according to Woram, are well suited for studio work and can be just as sturdy as the moving coils. Some feel that this variety of dynamic mic is warmer than a moving coil.

The pickup patterns

The omnidirectional

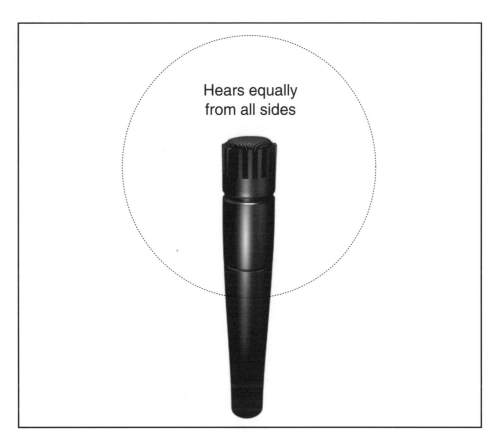

Hears equally
from all sides

The omnidirectional microphone has equal response at all angles. Its "coverage" or pickup angle is a full 360 degrees. This type of microphone can be used if more room ambience is desired. For example, when using an "omni," the balance of direct and ambient sound depends on the distance of the microphone from the instrument, and can be adjusted to the desired effect.

Unidirectional: cardioid, supercardioid and hypercardioid

Unidirectional microphones are available with several variations of the cardioid pattern. The unidirectional microphone is most sensitive to sound arriving from one particular direction and is less sensitive at other directions.

Cardioid

The most common type is a cardioid (heart-shaped) response. This has full sensitivity at 0 degrees (on-axis) and is least sensitive at 180 degrees (off-axis). Unidirectional microphones are used to isolate the desired on-axis sound from unwanted off-axis sound. In addition, the cardioid mic picks up only about one-third as much ambient sound as an omni.

Cardioid variations

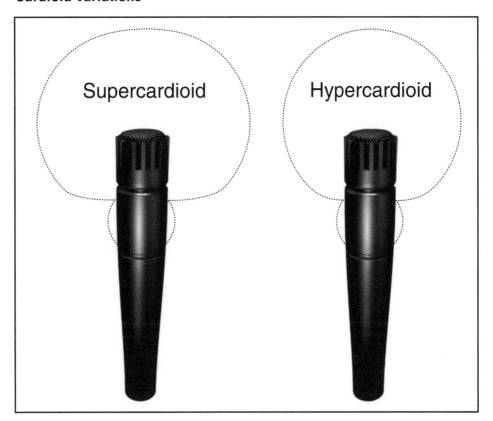

Two of these are the supercardioid and hypercardioid. Both patterns offer narrower front pickup angles than the cardioid (115 degrees for the supercardioid and 105 degrees for the hypercardioid) and also greater rejection of ambient sound. While the cardioid is least sensitive at the rear (180 degrees off-axis), the least sensitive direction is at 125 degrees for the supercardioid and 110 degrees for the hypercardioid. When placed properly they can provide more "focused" pickup and less room ambience than the cardioid pattern, but they have less rejection at the rear: -12 dB for the supercardioid and only -6 dB for the hypercardioid.

Bidirectional

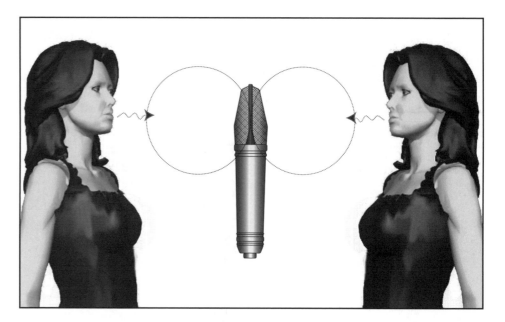

The bidirectional microphone has full response at both 0 degrees (front) and at 180 degrees (back). It has its least response at the sides. The coverage or pickup angle is only about 90 degrees at the front (or the rear). It has the same amount of ambient pickup as the cardioid. This mic could be used for picking up two sound sources such as two vocalists facing each other. It is also used in certain stereo techniques.

Other directional-related microphone characteristics

Ambient sound sensitivity - Since unidirectional microphones are less sensitive to off-axis sound than omnidirectional types, they pick up less overall ambient or room sound. Unidirectional mics should be used to control ambient noise pickup to get a "cleaner" recording.

Distance factor - Since directional microphones have more rejection of off-axis sound than omnidirectional types, they may be used at greater distances from a sound source and still achieve the same balance between the direct sound and background or ambient sound. An omnidirectional microphone will pick up more room (ambient) sound than a unidirectional microphone at the same distance. An omni should be placed closer to the sound source than a "uni"– about half the distance – to pick up the same balance between direct sound and room sound.

Off-axis coloration – A microphone's frequency response may not be uniform at all angles. Typically, high frequencies are most affected, which may result in an unnatural sound for off-axis instruments or room ambience.

Proximity effect - For most unidirectional types, bass response increases as the microphone is moved closer to the sound source. When miking close with unidirectional microphones (less than 1 foot), be aware of proximity effect: it may help to roll off the bass until you obtain a more natural sound. You can:

- Roll off low frequencies at the mixer
- Use a microphone designed to minimize proximity effect
- Use a microphone with a bass roll-off switch
- Use an omnidirectional microphone (which does not exhibit proximity effect)

Understanding and choosing the frequency response and directionality of microphones are selective factors which can improve pickup of desired sound and reduce pickup of unwanted sound. This can greatly assist in achieving both natural sounding recordings and unique sounds for special applications.

Next up

Very briefly, stereo miking.

Stereo Miking Techniques

One of the most popular specialized microphone techniques is stereo miking. This uses two or more microphones to create a stereo image often giving depth and spatial placement to an instrument or overall recording. There are three popular methods:

- The spaced pair (A/B)
- The coincident or near-coincident pair (X-Y configuration)
- The Mid-Side (M-S) technique

The spaced pair

The spaced pair (A/B) technique uses two cardioid or omnidirectional microphones spaced 3 - 10 feet apart from each other panned in left/right configuration to capture the stereo image of an ensemble or instrument.

Effective stereo separation is very wide. The distance between the two microphones is dependent on the physical size of the sound source. For instance, if two mics are placed ten feet apart to record an acoustic guitar; the guitar will appear in the center of the stereo image. This is probably too much spacing for such a small sound source. A closer, narrower mic placement should be used in this situation.

The drawback to A/B stereo miking is the potential for undesirable phase cancellation of the signals from the microphones. Due to the relatively large distance between the microphones and the resulting difference of sound arrival times at the microphones, phase cancellations and summing may be occurring. A mono reference source can be used to check for phase problems. When the program is switched to mono and frequencies jump out or fall out of the sound, you can assume that there is a phase problem. This may be a serious problem if your recording is going to be heard in mono as is typical in broadcast or soundtrack playback.

The X-Y technique

The X-Y technique uses two cardioid microphones of the same type and manufacture with the two mic capsules placed either as close as possible (coincident) or within 12 inches of each other (near-coincident) and facing each other at an angle ranging from 90 – 135 degrees, depending on the size of the sound source and the particular sound desired. The pair is placed with the center of the two mics facing directly at the sound source and panned left and right.

Because of the small distance between the microphones, sound arrives at the mics at nearly the same time, reducing (near coincident) or eliminating (coincident) the possible phase problems of the A/B techniques. The stereo separation of this technique is good but may be limited if the sound source is extremely wide. Mono compatibility is fair (near-coincident) to excellent (coincident).

Mid-Side stereo

The M-S or Mid-Side stereo technique involves a cardioid mic element and a bidirectional mic element, usually housed in a single case, mounted in a coincident arrangement. The cardioid (mid) faces directly at the source and picks up primarily on-axis sound while the bidirectional (side) faces left and right and picks up off-axis sound. The two signals are combined via the M-S matrix to give a variable controlled stereo image. By adjusting the level of mid versus side signals, a narrower or wider image can be created without moving the microphone. This technique is completely mono-compatible and is widely used in broadcast and film applications.

Conclusion

Needless to say, this is a very brief chapter on stereo recording, but enough to get you learning how to experiment once you get two mics.

For further reading

The Home Studio Guide to Microphones by Loren Alldrin

The Audio Pro Home Recording Course by Bill Gibson

Stereo Pickup Systems	Microphone Types	Microphone Positions	
X-Y	2-Cardiod	Axes of Maximum Response at 135° Spacing: Coincident	
ORTF (French Broadcasting Organization)	2-Cardiod	Axes of Maximum Response at 110° Spacing: Near Coincident (7 in.)	
NOS (Dutch Broadcasting Foundation)	2-Cardiod	Axes of Maximum Response at 90° Spacing: Near Coincident (12 in.)	
Stereosonic	2-Bidirectional	Axes of Maximum Response at 90° Spacing: Coincident	
MS (Mid-Side)	1-Cardiod 1-Bidirectional	Cardiod Forward-Pointed; Bidirectional Side-Pointed; Spacing: Coincident	
Spaced	2-Cardiod or 2-Omnidirectional	Angle as Desired Spacing: 3-10 ft.	

The Shure Gallery of Microphone Positions

In this chapter, we look at a series of mic positions in 3D derived from Shure's Microphone Techniques for Music Studio Recording with explanations and added instruction directly from it. Here, I've specifically focused on one and two mic positions for piano, amps, guitar, drums, vocalists and choir. John M. Woram in The Recording Studio Handbook pointed out that the law of correct microphone usage has been ignored since its discovery: Never use more than two mics. Woram explains that many sessions require multiple mics, but from a learning perspective, the budding engineer is best learning to work with no more than two before adding three or more. Thus, I've kept to this wise teaching throughout this chapter, until we get to the section on miking a choir. There, from Shure, I show a three mic setup.

Most of the illustrations are based around the Shure SM57, and therefore are specific to that mic. So what you're getting is very specific applied instruction. Again, a teaching reason. The Shure SM57 is the world's most used mic. It's also available for under $100 street price, thus making it financially accessible for many. For two mic setups, a little savings and with two Shure SM57's you're in business.

The second mic featured is the Shure Beta 91, which is a surface-mount mic used mostly to go inside bass drums, but also for recording pianos, which is how we're showing it here. It's a condenser mic with a cardiod pattern. The typical street price of a Beta 91 is around $225-$300.

One rule of thumb when using mic stands, ALWAYS make sure you position one of the legs under the mic boom to prevent toppling.

To state the obvious

I want to emphasize that these mic positions are starting points only, so lots of experimentation is needed before you get the "sound" you're looking for. One mic is connected to one channel strip. A second mic is connected to a second channel strip. In short, each mic to its own channel strip. Each channel strip records one mono audio track.

The Grand Piano

Here the mic is placed starting at 12 inches above the middle strings, 8 inches horizontally from the hammers with the lid off or at full stick. The tone is natural and well balanced. Move the microphone farther away from the hammers to reduce attack and mechanical noises. Listen to it from a number of positions, moving it slightly by an inch or two to see how this improves or degrades the sound depending on the room you're recording in.

The Grand Piano

This is a side shot of the microphone placed 12 inches above the middle strings and 8 inches horizontally from the hammers, as shown on the previous page.

The Grand Piano

Here the mic is placed next to the underside of the raised lid, centered on the lid and pointing down at the strings. This is an unobtrusive placement for the mic and gives a tonal balance that's bassy and full. John Woram reports that the open lid of the grand piano reflects both the piano sound and those of other instruments in the room. Thus, both wanted and unwanted reflections can be captured.

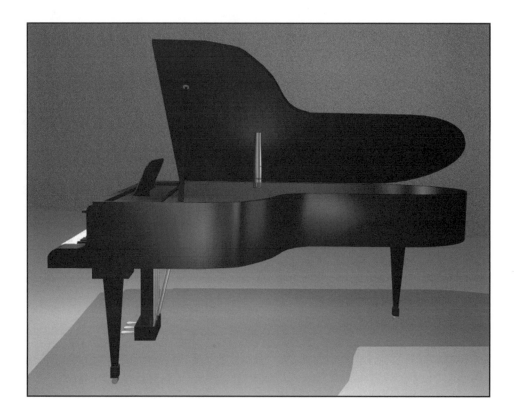

The Grand Piano

Here the mic is placed underneath the piano, aiming up at the soundboard. Again, this is an unobtrusive place to put the mic, but while the tone is bassy and full, it's also dull. Woram reports that most of the piano sound comes from its sounding board. From his perspective, there's little point in aiming the microphone(s) at the hammers. Woram's experience found that microphones can be placed under the piano, pointing up, or in the case of an upright piano, behind the piano. Both locations favor the sounding board, and may help keep unwanted reflections at a minimum.

The Grand Piano

The Beta 91 microphone is surface-mounted on the underside of the piano lid. It is positioned horizontally, over the treble strings. This gives excellent isolation and produces a bright, well-balanced tone. You can experiment with the lid height and mic placement to get your desired sound. Moving the microphone closer to the hammers will produce a brighter sound. Moving the mic further away from the hammers gives a more mellow sound. Woram discovered that a mic placed very close to the lid doesn't pick up as many reflections and favors the direct sound of the piano. The ideal placement depends on the lid's angle and the kind of music being recorded. As always, experiment.

Beta 91

The Grand Piano

This time, the Beta 91 is placed further back from the hammers, producing a more mellow sound that's less percussive.

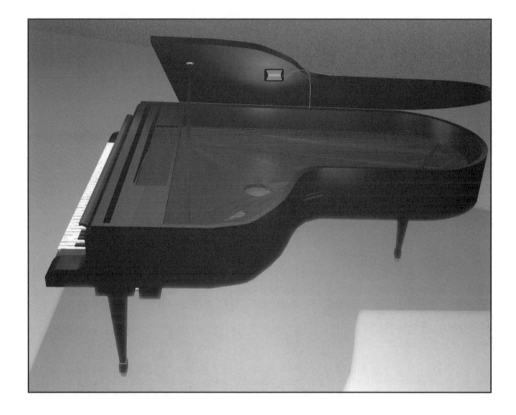

The Grand Piano

Here, the Beta 91 is surface-mounted in a vertical position on the inside of the piano frame, or rim, at or near the apex of the piano's curved wall. This is another position that gives excellent isolation. Both hammer and damper noise is minimized. This position produces a full, natural sound and works best if used in conjunction with two surface-mount microphones (like the Beta 91) mounted inside the closed lid.

These mics should be positioned at the keyboard edge of the closed lid, approximately 2/3 of the distance from middle A to each end of the keyboard. Moving the "low" end mic away from the keyboard 6 inches provides truer reproduction of the bass strings while reducing damper noise. By splaying these two mics outward slightly, the overlap in the middle registers can be minimized.

The Grand Piano

This mic is positioned 8 inches above the treble strings and 8 inches back from the hammers. The tone it produces is natural, well-balanced, and slightly bright.

The Grand Piano

This is a side shot of the mic, 8 inches above the treble strings and 8 inches back from the hammers. A shown on the previous page.

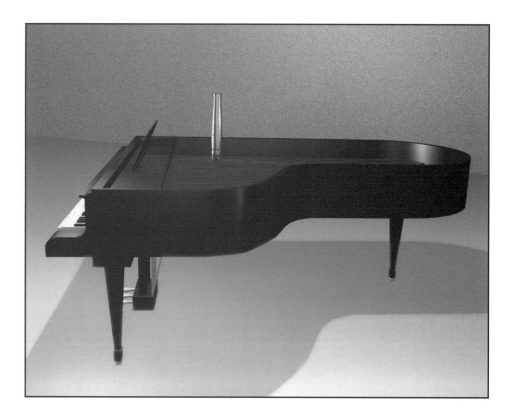

The Grand Piano

This is a stereo miking setup based on the previous mic position you saw. As before, one mic is positioned 8 inches above the treble strings and 8 inches back from the hammers. Now place a second mic 8 inches above the bass strings and 8 inches back from the hammers. This is called a spaced pair technique. The tonal balance is natural, well-balanced, and slightly bright. However, be aware that phase cancellations may occur if the recording is heard in mono.

The Electric Guitar, Bass or Keyboard Amp

The mic is placed 3 feet from the center of the speaker cone. It can yield a thin, reduced bass, and picks up more room ambiance and leakage. Move the mic and notice how the sound changes. For a more "rock" sound, put the mic right on the grille. For a mellower sound, begin moving back, usually no more than six feet. Though not pictured, you can also use a two-mic approach with one mic close to the grille and the other up to six feet back.

The Electric Guitar, Bass or Keyboard Amp

This is an overhead shot of the mic position 3 feet from the center of the speaker cone. Earlier I taught that keyboards, samplers and other MIDI gear can be connected directly to the mixing board. But you can also run them through amps, record them with a mic and get a warmer, more natural sound. Experiment. For keyboard amps, mic back a little farther than normal. Again, experiment.

The Electric Guitar, Bass or Keyboard Amp

The mic is placed about 4 inches from the grille cloth at the center of the speaker cone. This produces a natural, well-balanced tone. A small microphone desk stand may be used if the loud speaker is close to the floor. For bass amps, many engineers recommend using a dynamic mic placed 8-12 inches away from the grille.

The Electric Guitar, Bass or Keyboard Amp

This is an overhead shot of the mic placed 4 inches from the center of the speaker cone.

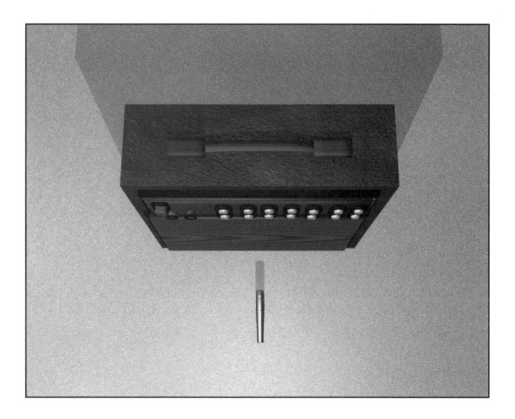

The Electric Guitar, Bass or Keyboard Amp

The mic is placed three inches from the grille cloth but off-center with respect to the speaker cone. The tone is dull or mellow. Placing the mic closer to the edge of the speaker cone results in a duller (darker) sound but reduces amplifier hiss noise. Working off axis affects brightness. Again, experiment.

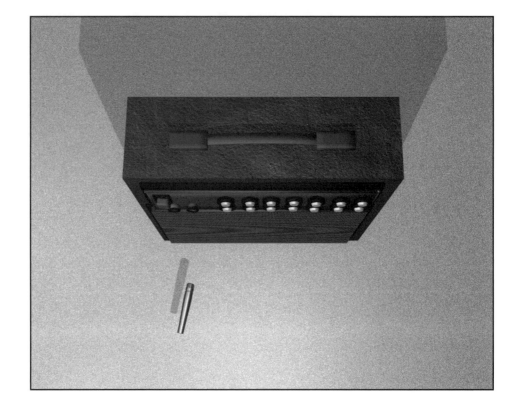

The Electric Guitar, Bass or Keyboard Amp

The mic is placed one inch from the grille cloth at the center of the speaker cone. This position minimizes feedback and leakage. The tone is bassy. With a guitar, you can get a more "fat" sound.

The Electric Guitar, Bass or Keyboard Amp

This is an overhead shot of the mic placed one inch from the grille cloth at the center of the speaker cone. For a more "live" sound, record the bass direct to the board from the amp on one track, and "live" with the mic in front of the amp for the other track. The direct line yields the lows while the miked yields the highs.

The Acoustic Guitar

The mic is placed 8 inches from the sound hole. This is a good starting placement when leakage is a problem. The tone is dark and bassy so you may need to roll off some of the bass for a more natural sound. Both condenser and dynamic mics can be used, but the condenser gives the most detailed sound.

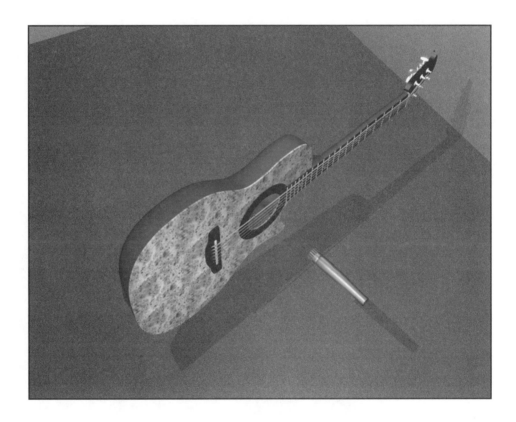

The Acoustic Guitar

The mic is placed 8-12 inches away to the right of the sound-hole. This position gives you clean highs, but can become thin and tinny-sounding as you move further up the neck. Be aware that you'll also pick up more string and finger noise using this mic position. If the guitar sounds too small, move it towards the body. If it's too big, move it towards the fretboard.

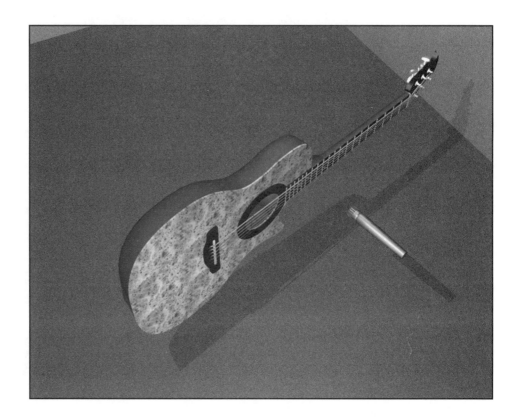

The Acoustic Guitar

The mic is placed 4-8 inches from the bridge. This position reduces pick and string noise. The tone is woody, warm and mellow but is mid-bassy and lacks detail. There's not as much definition to the notes.

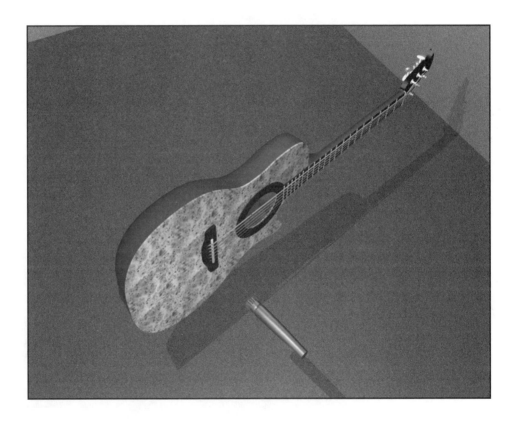

The Drum Kit

The drum kit is one of the most complicated sound sources to record. Although there are many different methods, some common techniques and principles should be understood. Since the different parts of the drum kit have widely varying sound, they should be considered as individual instruments, or at least a small group of instrument types: Kick, Snare, Toms, Cymbals, and Percussion. Certain mic characteristics are extremely critical for drum usage.

A drum can produce very high Sound Pressure Levels (SPLs). The microphone must be able to handle these levels. A dynamic microphone will usually handle high SPLs better than a condenser. Check the maximum SPL in condenser microphone specifications. It should be at least 130dB for closeup drum use.

This picture shows 2 mics positioned level with the drummer's ears and pointing towards the front of the kit.

The Drum Kit

This mic is positioned about 6 feet above the floor and behind the kit, or a foot or two above the drummer's head. It's directly over the drummer's head, pointed at the set.

The Drum Kit

This mic is positioned about 6 feet above the floor in front of the kit, pointed at the set. Mic distance affects room ambience recorded along with the type of pickup pattern the mic uses.

The Drum Kit

This mic is positioned about eight feet from the kit, pointed at the drums. Again, mic distance affects room ambience recorded along with the type of pickup pattern the mic uses.

The Drum Kit

Here is another one mic position, about four feet above the drummer's head. Again, mic distance affects room ambience recorded along with the type of pickup pattern the mic uses. For this technique, some engineers suggest using a cardioid or hypercardioid pattern to reduce the amount of recorded room ambience.

The Drum Kit

This is a two mic setup with one overhead and one in the bass drum. The bass drum mic is placed inside the kick, aimed at the head, about half-way between the center of the head and the shell. Padding is often placed inside the bass drum to help deaden its sound. Because of the intense sound pressure levels inside the kick, you'll need a sturdy mic. A dynamic mic will work well, giving a warm, full sound. If you can't remove the head of your bass drum to place a mic inside, you'll need to mic it from the outside of the drum. This mic placement will give you a softer, more mellow sound. Woram reports that the front (resonant) head of the bass drum is removed, with a blanket stuffed inside the drum, against the batter head (where the bass drum beater strikes). This seems to produce a more percussive attack. Try positioning the mic inside the bass drum away from the batter head, closer to the shell, etc.

The Drum Kit

This is a stereo two mic XY overhead setup, also known as coincident miking. The mics are positioned three feet above the cymbals at a 90 degree angle to each other, pointing at the center of the kit. The mics should be positioned so that they pivot on the same imaginary axis. This gives a very precise stereo image. It's best to use mics with cardioid, supercardioid or hypercardioid patterns. Tighter patterns allow for greater angles between mics. Again, experiment.

The Drum Kit

This is an overhead view of the stereo two mic XY overhead setup. It's considered a good setup for jazz and pop music. If possible, try adding a third mic to the bass drum for better balance when mixing.

The Vocalist

This is a typical studio setup for either a singer or a spoken word recording. In front of the singer/actor is a wind screen, also called a pop filter, which helps to de-pop the "puhh" sound you hear with words starting with the letters p and b. This sound is called a plosive. Singers and actors have varying vocal qualities. The task is to position the mic, through trial and success, to get the best tonal quality of the voice. Start the mic positioning at the center of the mouth. Then move it up, then down, until the best location is found. Depending on the mic, you may have to move it closer. Some engineers recommend using an omnidirectional mic to reduce the popping noises.

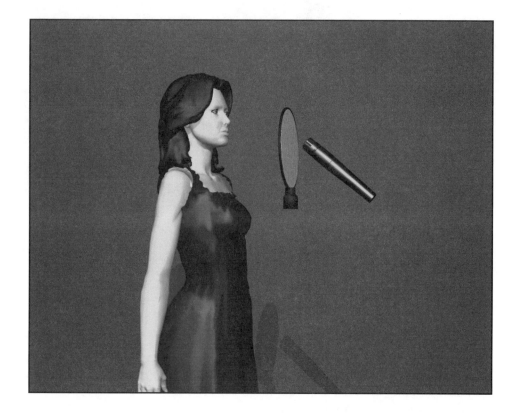

The Vocalist

This is a "live" setup for either a singer or a spoken word performance (like acting, reading, preaching, etc.) Here, the pop filter is removed and any wind screen used will be on the mic. If the room is really "live" you'll need to put the mic closer.

The Vocalist

Moving the vocalist towards or away from a harder surface can affect the sound drastically because the reflections of the voice against the surface changes the voice's texture. Body movements also affect vocal consistency.

The Vocalist

Where you place the mike in relation to the singer will affect the tonal quality of the singer's voice. With the mic aimed directly at the singer's mouth, you'll get a pretty even tonal balance, but breaths, sniffs and other mouth noises, etc., will also come through loud and clear. A good starting position is directly in front of the mouth about half a foot to a foot away. For a softer sound, try moving the mic to the side of the singer's mouth.

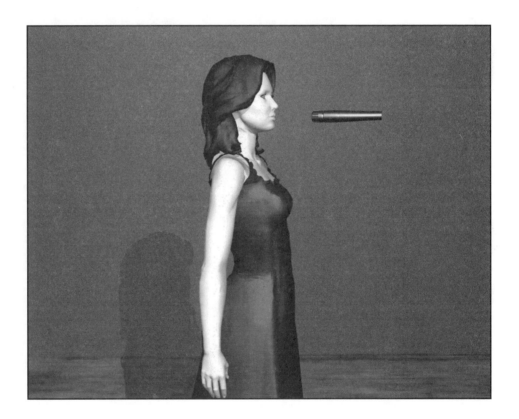

The Vocalist

If you can't get a good sound by placing the mic directly in front of the singer's mouth, try moving the mic up about three or four inches and pointing it down at the singer's mouth. This will eliminate a lot of unwanted sounds like breaths, sniffs and other mouth noises. This mic position is a great one to use if you want to lessen the nasal quality of a singer's voice.

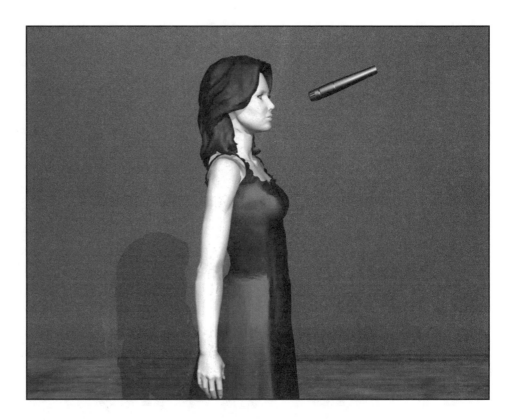

The Vocalist

If you're recording a singer with a thin sounding voice, you can try moving the mic down four to six inches below the singer's mouth, then aiming the mic up at the mouth. This can help fill out a singer's tone, but you may pick up a lot of unwanted noise. This mic position is not advisable for singer's with a nasal tone.

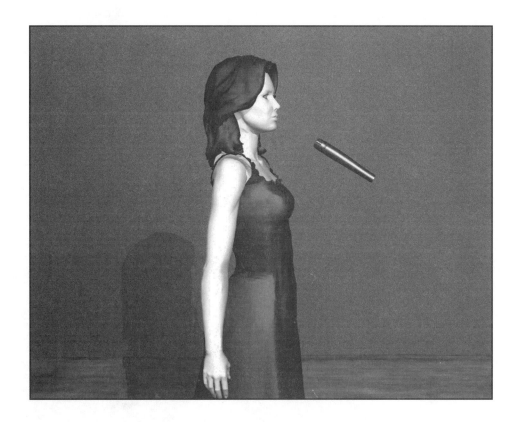

The Choir

Application of choir microphones falls into the category known as "area" coverage. Rather than one microphone per sound source, the object is to pick up multiple sound sources (or a "large" sound source) with one (or more) microphone(s).

If a choir is a single large entity, and it becomes necessary to choose sections based solely on the coverage of the individual microphones, use the following spacing: one microphone for each lateral section of approximately 6 to 9 feet. If the choir is unusually deep (more than 6 to 8 rows), it may be divided into two vertical sections of several rows each, with aiming angles adjusted accordingly. In any case, **it is better to use too few microphones than too many**.

To determine the microphone placement of multiple microphones for choir pickup, remember the following rules: observe the 3-to-1 rule which says that when using multiple mics, the distance between mics should be at least three times the distance from each mic to its intended sound source; avoid picking up the same sound source with more than one microphone; and finally, use the minimum number of microphones.

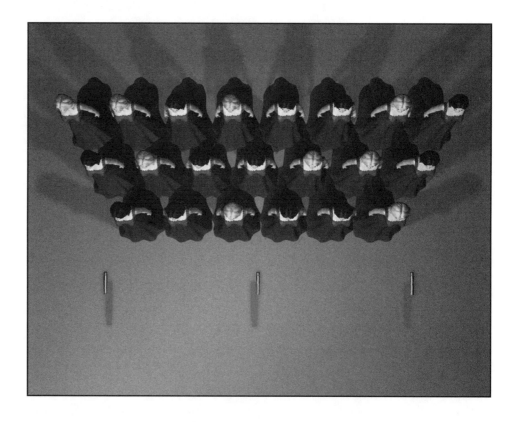

The Choir

For multiple microphones, the objective is to divide the choir into sections that can each be covered by a single microphone. If the choir has any existing physical divisions, (aisles or boxes) use these to define basic sections. If the choir is grouped according to vocal range (soprano, alto, tenor, bass), these may serve as sections.

In this side shot, the mics are angled at 2-3 feet above the heads of the back row aimed at the heads, then positioned 2-3 feet ahead of the front row.

Conclusion

Throughout this chapter, one word stood out - experiment. I want to restate that these are starting positions. The sound you get depends on the room you're recording in, your recorder, the mic, the mic's pickup pattern, where it's placed, the musician, the singer, the instrument, the mixing board, the amp, weather, the sound of the room, noise outside the room (especially if you're recording at home), etc., etc., etc!

There's no canned answer. You learn by doing. And the final arbiter is your hearing. No machine or device pops up a flag that says, "This one!" Only your ears can do that. The more you do it, the more you learn. Oh, and by the way, no matter what you do, everyone *will* have an opinion as to what sounds best. At that point, you listen, consider, and then make your own decision, because it's your work and you're responsible.

Finally!
Now You Can Record!

At this point, you've now learned enough facts of recording to begin doing your own live recording. You've learned about studios and thoughts on how you do home recording. You've learned about connectors and cables, connectors on the recorder, connectors on things that connect to the board, how to connect to the mixing board, signal flow, connecting effects boxes, signal flow in virtual mixing boards, and finally mics and mic positions.

Wow! That's a lot!

If you know the basic operations of your recorder and you have a mic, you're ready to go.

Now, to set your expectations.

The most important thing you can do right now is approach recording with the attitude of learning and acquiring skills. In short, ya gotta have fun with this. If you approach this with the mindset that every recording must be an award level session, you will not only miss out on a lot, you ultimately will quit because you're not having any fun with it. If you wait until you've learned every possible recording option before you make an actual recording, you'll never get a recording done. The thing to focus on is learning mic techniques and how to get a good sound.

Any focus beyond that for today is too focused.

Arranging and recording

A well designed arrangement for your song makes recording a lot easier. Do you know about and understand song form? If not, then you need to read Sheila Davis' *The Craft of Lyric Writing* to learn how a song is organized. Once you understand that, you have the basics on how to analytically listen to a song to write down section by section how the song is arranged, where the soloists come in, how choruses and bridges are handled, and so much more. A well arranged song compensates for lack of recording experience.

Get going!

I don't want to say any more than this for right now. So get that mic and start recording. After you've gotten your feet wet a few times, go to the next chapter and learn more about mixing and panning.

Setting Panning & Volume Levels From Within the Software & the Board

A typical definition of panning is, "where a sound is placed in the stereo spectrum." This is a good working definition, but it doesn't really tell us what we want to accomplish in reality. At a more basic level, I'd like to offer this panning definition that fits more into what we need to accomplish in a MIDI or audio mix:

> *Panning is the art of recording the feel of the instrumental/vocal positioning of a live performance.*

This definition can vary depending on the kind of music you're doing, but in general, this definition defines the end result that you want to get to. This means defining where each instrumental voice is placed so that it has its own place and space in the mix whether you're recording in a sequencer or an independent recorder.

How you set the panning

When talking about Panning, you always talk in terms of "positions." The three broadest panning positions are center, hard left, and hard right. Panning can be done at the mixer, in the sequencer, or at the keyboard! To complicate matters, each manufacturer has a different range for executing panning.

The MIDI of panning

Because panning is a MIDI controller function, most keyboards, samplers, sound modules, etc., can both transmit and receive panning positions via MIDI. Virtual mixing boards panning and volume levels are controlled by MIDI. This means that you can alter the pan positions of individual channels in a mix using a sequencing program such as Cubase, Emagic Logic, Cakewalk, or Samplitude.

Panning information is transmitted on MIDI Controller #10.

Panning from within a software program

When sending panning information to a keyboard from a sequencing program you need to be aware of the distinction between fine and coarse panning positions. Korg units, which typically pan from 0 to -9 on the left and 0 to -9 on the right use coarse panning, as do the Roland samplers with their 0 to 32 range.

By comparison, a software sequencer gives you fine panning. This means you can set panning within 63 positions left and 63 positions right. That's because panning as a MIDI controller generally ranges between 0 and 127, where 0 = hard left, 127 = hard right, and 64 = center.

Each software company defines the panning range of their sequencing programs differently. This applies to MIDI and the virtual board.

Sequencer	Hard Left	Center	Hard Right
Cubase	L64	Off or 0	R63
Logic	0	64	127
Cakewalk	0	64	127

In Piano roll edit when sequencing, these values can change. For example, in Cubase hard left now = 0, center = 64, and hard right = 127.

When you set the panning up manually within a keyboard, it's in a fixed position, in that you'll have to physically go into the editing pages of the keyboard to alter the sound's pan position to a different setting, not very convenient when you're trying to play at the same time! But by setting the keyboard's pan positions from a sequencing program, the panning can change and even be automated.

Each sequencing program defines what an individual "sequence" is differently:

Cakewalk = clip

Cubase = part

Emagic = sequence

Samplitude 2496 = object

Each of these programs lets you assign the pan position for each recorded sequence and audio track. So, each individual clip/part/sequence/object can have a different panning position. Not that you'd want to, but you can.

Look at this example from the sequencing program Cubase and look for the pan element in the Inspector area. This is where you can go to set the pan position for each individual "part."

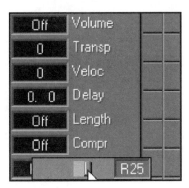

In piano roll edit you can draw in special panning effects like random panning of individual notes in a melody to different positions in the stereo spectrum, creating a scattered effect. Or you could set up an instrument so that the melody slowly pans across the stereo field from the left speaker to the right, then moves to the center. The possibilities are vast.

What you'll pan & where

Where you're going to pan your instruments to depends on the kind of ensemble you're writing for. You need to visualize where each musician would be sitting on stage in a live performance, then you'll set your panning positions to recreate those seating positions for each instrument. A good way to visualize your panning positions is to draw a stage layout of the ensemble you're recording.

Danger!

The default panning position in sequencing programs and many units is the center position. The problem with that setting is that all the sound is in the same location. No one sound has a spot of its own. Just as no two people can occupy the same space at the same time, neither can two performers! The way you set your panning positions helps to create a sense of space in the mix.

Symphony orchestra setup

Strings

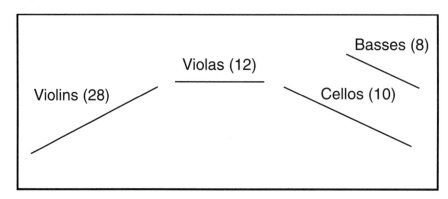

Now where most people make their mistake with strings is that they automatically assume, pan hard left/hard right. And at first glance, that does make sense. Except! That the string section sound has four parts to it: violins, violas (a more nasal sound), cellos (deep and rich), and the basses (depth). So you'll want to separate these out by panning them to different positions in your sequencing program as follows:

Instrument	Position
Violins	hard left
Violas	center
Cellos	mid right
Basses	hard right

Then you have to balance your levels. Eight basses are not going to over-power 28 violins! So you have to set your volume levels accordingly (See later in this chapter).

Now, you can achieve a similar effect with two strings Programs. Pick one for the low strings (violas to basses) and pan as above. Pick a second one for the violins and pan as above. Create a pad for the low strings (3-4 note chord) and then bring the melody in on the left in the upper register. That's a powerful sound and everything cuts through.

Woodwinds

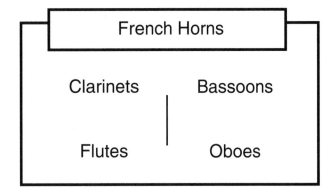

The little vertical line in the box indicates the center position. Flutes and clarinets are slightly to the left of center. Oboes (English horn) and bassoons (contrabassoons) are slightly to the right of center. Pan them in your sequencer as follows.

Instrument	Position
French horns	center
Clarinets	soft left
Flute	soft left
Bassoons	soft right
Oboes	soft right

1. When the flute is in unison with the clarinet, the flute will be a little louder in level than the clarinet since the clarinet sits behind the flute.

2. When the flute is in unison with the oboe, the levels will be about the same because they're next to each other.

3. When the clarinet is in unison with the oboe, the clarinet will be a little softer in level than the oboe since the oboe sits in front.

4. When the flute is in octaves with the bassoon, the flute will slightly predominate.

5. French horns traditionally sit directly behind the woodwinds. Because the bells are pointed to the back, their sound is less. At *f*, it takes two French horns to equal the power of one trumpet. Often in studio sessions, the French horns will sit slightly to the left, especially if six to eight are used for the session.

Brass

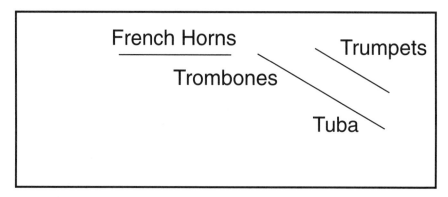

With three- to four-part harmony, trombones and tuba are on the right. When the French horns are added in for a low pad with the trombones, the spread is similar to the violas and cellos.

Because the French horns don't have the power of the trumpets and trombones, they're set off to the side so they cut through. Good brass writing frequently has the trombones and trumpets sustaining, while the French horns play soli unencumbered from the rest of the section. Pan them in your sequencer as follows.

Instrument	Position
French horns	center
Trombones	soft right
Trumpets	mid right
Tuba	mid right

The basic pop setup chart

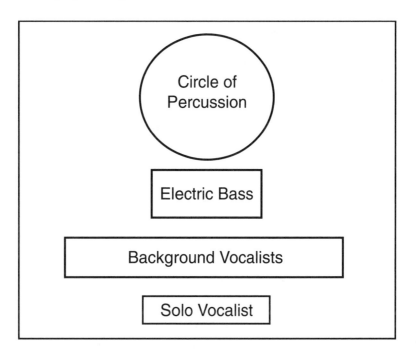

You can listen to dozens of cuts and you'll hear this set up over and over again. So let's go over it.

1. The solo vocalist is up front, center (usually panned stereo hard left and right). Dynamically, the solo voice predominates. *Everything* is slightly below it in dynamics.

2. If there are background vocalists, their volume will be lower than the soloist (unless intentionally desired otherwise) and the panning is closer to 10 o' clock left, and 2 o' clock right. Only by experimentation and intense listening will you know if you should pan in full stereo. There's no formula. You just have to experiment.

3. Next is the bass guitar. It's going to be louder than the bass drum. Again, panned center.

4. Here's why I call it the circle of percussion: the snare drum and bass drum are both dead center. But the hi-hat, top toms, floor toms and cymbals are all in different positions. Different percussion sounds are to the left and right of center.

What about the rest of the band?

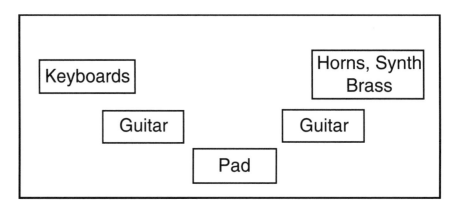

So what's missing is the lead guitar, rhythm guitar, horns, pad and keyboards.

The Pad - Its purpose is often to outline the melody for the solo vocalist. It can be a pad sound, a string sound, etc. It's going to be behind the solo vocalist and lower in volume. Hence, the middle position. It's often made up of whole notes and half notes. And frequently just plays the chords. Where the chords fall is called the harmonic rhythm of the piece.

The Guitars - So far, everything is in the center. Now we give some space to the guitars. Depending on the project, you can position the rhythm guitar on the right and the lead on the left, or reverse them. It all depends on the kind of ensemble you set up.

Brass - You can switch this position with the keyboards. For a starting position, however, especially with a trumpet-like brass section, it's traditional to keep it on the right. If, however, your brass sound is more French horn-like, switch with the keyboards and move it to the left.

Keyboards - This doesn't have to be a pad sound. It could be electric piano playing fillers behind the pad, bell-like sounds, harp-like sounds, etc. In the orchestra, keyboards and harp are positioned on the left in front, letting them cut through the whole ensemble.

The whole set up would use these positions in your sequencing program:

Instrument	Position
Solo vocal	center
Background vocals	soft left
Background vocals	soft right
Bass guitar	center
Drum set	center
The Pad	center
Lead guitar	mid left
Rhythm guitar	mid right
Brass: trumpets	hard right
Brass: French horns	hard left
Keyboards	hard left

The big band or large jazz ensemble

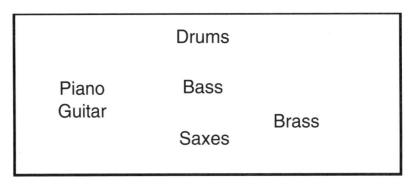

This is a very basic setup for a "studio approach." The drums, bass and saxes are panned center, with the brass to the right and the piano and guitar to the left. The saxophones will have the main presence, so they go up front. Pan them in your sequencer as follows:

Instrument	Position
Drums	center
Bass	center
Saxes	center
Brass	mid right
Piano	mid left
Guitar	mid left

Understanding levels

Any discussions we have about volume all have one end in mind: setting up a preliminary working mix as a prelude to the final mix. If you don't do that in the beginning, you just spend lots of wasted time later on. When we talk about volume, we must also consider instrumental volume and dynamics within each instrument's specific range.

Our goal in setting up a MIDI mix is to replicate that which happens in nature. We're not dealing with real instruments. We're dealing with digital snapshots of a musical moment captured in time. If you don't know how loud something is, or is supposed to be, you can't effectively set the volume levels within your mix. A good way of developing your listening skills is to use study scores and listen to CDs as a way to benchmark and compare your work.

Musical issues behind setting levels (how loud is loud?)

Dynamics

It doesn't really matter what kind of music you're looking to do. All music has dynamic and volume issues. Dynamics let the music breathe and have life whereas maintaining a dynamic level can not only be overpowering at times, but confusing since the ear doesn't know where to focus. Shown below are the various dynamic markings and their corresponding levels.

Dynamic	Level
ppp	extremely quiet
pp	very quiet
p	quiet
mp	moderately quiet
mf	moderately loud
f	loud
ff	very loud
fff	extremely loud

When writing music whose dynamic range stretches from very quiet to very loud, you have to first decide where *ff* is, then determine where *pp* will be, as this is the quietest dynamic for the whole piece. What we're looking at is building to a volume principle, but the dynamic volume settings are heavily dependent on the instrument(s) and what combination they happen to be in.

f for a whole string section vs. *f* for the brass section are two very different *f*s! A brass section at *f* can wipe out the strings! You sense the presence of the strings, but the brass dominate.

Another practical example.

How loud are pizzicato strings at *f* compared to brass at *f*? To not overpower the pizzicato strings, you might have to set the brass at *mf* or even *mp* depending on the passage. Now, if the brass are in the lead and the pizzicato strings are supporting the brass, that's a different story, because what you're doing is creating, to use a synth term, a layering effect with the orchestra.

The composer in his mind must work this out, but the conductor in the rehearsal and actual performance makes it happen. *You are both!* And your rehearsal is the pre-mix with the MIDI mix being the actual performance.

Rimsky-Korsakov and the French school of orchestration

In his landmark book on orchestration, Rimsky-Korsakov set forth sonic principles which are still true today. The French adapted Rimsky's principles and pushed them to new limits with much of the music written at the beginning of the 20th century. Recordings can be quite deceptive. Here are the dynamic principles that Rimsky-Korsakov observed.

In a f passage:

> 1 trumpet = 1 trombone = 1 tuba = 2 French horns
>
> Woodwinds are 1/4 the volume of the brass and 1/2 the volume of the French horns.
>
> 1 horn = 2 clarinets = 2 oboes = 2 flutes = 2 bassoons
>
> Violins 1 or Violins 2 = 1 horn = 2 woodwind instruments

In a p passage, all wind and brass instruments are of fairly equal balance.

> Violin 1 or Violin 2 = 1 woodwind instrument
>
> Woodwinds thicken strings, soften brass
>
> When two or more woodwinds are combined with one string section, the woodwinds absorb the strings and begin to predominate.

The French school of orchestration took these principles to heart. If you look at Ravel's work (especially Mother Goose Suite, La Valse, Bolero), you'll hear all kinds of instrumental colors and interplay. These are all balanced by Ravel writing much of his music between pp and mf.

Thus the orchestration principles you can learn from Ravel, Debussy and others are immediately adaptable to MIDI scoring and mixing. From a MIDI perspective, the orchestra now becomes a rich source of combinations and performances.

Velocity vs. Loudness

Velocity controls the intensity with which you strike the MIDI keyboard. Its range is from either 0 to 127 or 1 to 128 depending on the keyboard or module you're using.

When we talk about intensity, we're talking about the force with which you strike the keyboard. That force is musically defined with words like staccato, accented, separated, forte, piano, and mezzopiano.

We need to clarify at this point that velocity is not volume. It has to do with volume, but it's separate. Volume has to do with loudness. Intensity has to do with phrasing and shaping the melodic line.

Intensity (or velocity) is the way in which you perform a piece of music. The higher the velocity, the more intense the performance. The lower the velocity, the less intense the performance. Here's an experiment you might want to try, to familiarize yourself with the way instruments respond to changes in velocity and to show you that intensity (velocity) is not volume. Changing the velocity is changing the feel of a performance.

1. Pick a sound from your keyboard that has a wide dynamic range, like a piano.

2. In your sequencer, record a short musical passage at *pp* performing a crescendo up to *ff*. Look at the Event list to see how the velocity readings changed, along with the length of the notes played as your keyboard touch becomes more intense.

3. Now reverse it. Go from *ff* to *pp*. Look at the Event list to see how the velocity readings changed.

4. Now do four notes crescendo from *pp* to *mf*, then diminuendo from *mf* to *pp* for the next group of four. Repeat the whole phrase. Look at the Event list to see how the velocity readings changed.

Intensity and the harmonic overtone series

So far, we've discussed intensity as a keyboard performance. There is another factor that must be kept in mind, especially as we look at volume. With an acoustic instrument that's blown, plucked or bowed, the higher the pitch, the higher it is on the harmonic overtone series. The result is more intense sound because it's either at a higher position on the string or requires more breath to play.

The challenge for the performer is to practice his dynamics so that as he goes higher, and the intensity increases, his volume doesn't get loud just because he's playing higher. That's the natural tendency. The more musical performance can have astonishing highs played softly.

Of course that depends on the instrument and the performer too. And admittedly, this is an orchestration issue, but one you should keep in mind as you listen to and edit sounds that are emulations of acoustic instruments.

Setting volume levels from within a sequencer

Just like panning, volume is also a MIDI controller function that keyboards can transmit and receive via MIDI. Using sequencing programs such as Emagic Logic, Cubase, Cakewalk etc. you can set and change the volume levels of Programs assigned to different channels in a mix.

Whereas volume levels set within your keyboard are fixed, programming volume changes using an external sequencer lets you have more freedom. For example, you can program crescendos and diminuendos.

Volume information is transmitted on MIDI Controller #7.

But before you begin...

You need to set the volume level at your mixing board.

Establishing unity gain at the mixing board

When you're using a mixing board, you're going to set the volume between the mixing board and your sequencing program.

First, your volume levels on your MIDI equipment need to be all the way up. This insures that the signal is "hot" enough. To begin, you want to first set the Unity Gain levels, also called 0dB. This concept is also called zeroing out the board.

You start by setting each of the faders on the mixing board at the 'U' position (Unity Gain). Look for the meter bridge on your board. If it doesn't have one, look at the meter section of the board. Select the Program from the keyboard you want to use in your sequencer. Tap your keyboard and see if the volume levels are above or below the Unity Gain setting. Then look for what's called the trim or gain knob at the top of the channel strip of the mixing board. Adjust until the signal is hitting consistently at the 0dB (Unity Gain) level.

Repeat this procedure for every unit in your recording.

Now do it for vocalists, instrumentalists, etc.

Where are levels within a sequencer controlled?

This is a thorny question. Every program or sample is going to have its own recorded level. You adjust unity gain at the mixing board, but that doesn't mean that the samples are at blendable dynamic levels. For example, with a strings sample, that single sample may reflect 14 violins. The bass sample may reflect six basses. Six basses won't overpower 14 violins! And if you're recreating a section, you're talking about 28 violins, maybe 10 violas and 10-12 cellos. You see, immediately you're involved with pre-mixing and panning. Now, where and how is that reflected? At the sequencer? At the mixing board? And what happens when you're using two or more samples to create a single sound? Are they blended in the sequencing program or at the board?

Well, it depends on your sequencing program and if you have a digital board with automated faders. Overall, it's best to set Unity Gain at the mixing board and keep it there. Then, adjust your dynamic levels within the sequencer.

Setting the Main Volume For Each Track

To set the main track volume in your sequencing program you need to play the keyboard and set the maximum volume level for each track. Track by track you define where *f* is. Expect it to be different for each track.

Once you've done this you're now doing a MIDI mix within your sequencer and mixing as you go!

Look at this example from the sequencing program Cubase and look for the 'Volume' element in the Inspector area. This is where you can go to set the volume for each individual part.

In piano roll edit you can draw in volume changes. This is a quick and easy way to add crescendos and diminuendos to your mix plus other customized volume effects.

Conclusion

If you're recording a few people, panning and volume levels are much easier to control. The minute you add in synths and samplers for a bigger production, the issues grow exponentially, especially when you're trying to create a single sound from combining synths or samplers together. Nonetheless, the principles here remain the same. How they're applied with each unit or software program is an operations issue to be defined and learned.

Mixing: Part 2
Reverb & Effects

Part of mixing is learning how to use and apply effects. In this chapter, I've focused on four effects: reverb, EQ, delay and compression. Learn to master these four and you can handle most recording situations. If you've got a digital audio recorder or a sequencing/digital audio program, most likely you have all these effects just waiting for you. What you have to remember is that learning to use effects, like developing good mic skills, comes from using your ears. With effects, you're either placing a sound in a room (reverb) or changing the sound in some way by using reverb and the other effects. You can change the sound to enhance it or completely change it. When you're completely changing it you're doing sound design.

About learning effects

Working with effects is an ear training affair. You learn what the various effects sound like starting with the factory presets and then apply them. Next is learning the controls and from there, learning how to make adjustments. So my approach here is to just cover the four most basic effects and then have you apply them using the factory presets of your host software or digital unit. For a book, that's as far as we can go.

Two ways to apply effects

There are two ways to apply effects. The first is "live" where the performer and effects are recorded as one. This can be for either live performance or for recording purposes. This way, you know what the final result is going to sound like before you record it. The second is after the audio is recorded, and the effect is applied within the digital audio program or unit. Here, you build the sound after it's recorded.

Where placed

There are two basic locations. For music recording, reverb is connected to the the aux sends and returns and for special usage, on the channel inserts. It could also be placed on the master outs.

In a virtual board or digital unit, the EQ is an effect and appears as a channel insert. In all other hardware boards, it's part of each channel strip.

Compression and delay are usually applied at the channel inserts, however, delay could be used on the aux sends. Compression can also be applied at the master outs.

Reverb

Summarizing from John Woram, reverb is a re-echoed sound with many repetitions.

The purpose of reverb is to place the sound in a room that simulates its natural acoustics. With close miking, because the distance is so short between the performer and the mic, there's almost no natural acoustic phenomenon happening. So adding reverb adds a room acoustic, warming up the sound and making it less sterile sounding. For home recording, if you're recording in a carpeted room, the carpet can absorb the higher frequencies while glass can reflect them. Reverbs are usually named to described specific types of rooms being electronically emulated. These are room (small, medium and large), hall (small, large, grand), Cathedral (standard, large and huge), sometimes church. You also have the options, in some reverb presets, of having bright and dark presets.

Halls

Large halls have superb natural acoustics because they used materials that naturally reflected the sound. Says John Woram in *The Recording Studio Handbook*, "In the older concert halls, one often finds mirrored walls, paneling, thick plaster surfaces and perhaps parqueted wood floors - all of which reflect sound and contribute to that illusive concert hall realism." How the sound is heard depends on where the listener sits. If he sits up front, he hears mostly (what Woram calls) the direct signal. If the listener is sitting in the back then he hears, "...a signal that is almost totally reflected sounds."

In using the factory settings of reverb, start first with dry and then apply the reverb to make the sound more wet. The more dry, the closer to the "signal" you are. The more wet, the further back in the hall you are. At a hardware mixing board, you set that up at the aux sends and returns. For virtual boards, it can be a place labeled aux sends (as in Samplitude), or a bus (as in Logic). It all depends on the program. Same for digital units. You have to find where the aux sends and returns are in the software, apply the effect starting dry then adding in more.

Note:

The best way to understand this is go to a symphony concert that has the same performances for two nights. On the first night, get tickets to sit close to the orchestra (expensive). On the second night, get tickets that seat you in the rear or the balcony (cheap). Mentally compare the difference in sound.

Note:

Let's say you're working with string and orchestra samples. The more wet the reverb, the further back in the hall you're putting the listener. The more dry they are, the closer to orchestra the listener of your music is sitting.

Understand that whatever instrument you pick out in this hall, it will have the illusion of sounding like it is being played in a large symphonic hall.

Stage

This simulates the acoustic characteristics of a club.

Room

This simulates the characteristics of semi-dry room.

Plate

In large studios, a device was created using a large suspended steel plate that when carefully positioned, helped simulate the natural reverberant sound of a concert hall. So think of the plate reverb as another type of hall reverb. You'll often find this as a reverb preset.

Spring

Again, found in studios, this is a device that uses springs to simulate the reverberant sound of a concert hall. You'll often find this as a reverb preset.

Reverb controls

The basic controls of all reverbs are:

Room size - some add a Room Shape selection, too.

Mix - adjusts the amount of reverb you add (wet or dry).

Pre-delay - determines the point in time when the actual reverb effect will begin in relationship to the source signal being input (TC Works definition).

To illustrate, I've chosen the reverb from TC Works Native Bundle because it has the most standard controls and reverb names are consistent with industry practice. TC Works also adds three room shapes to choose from (round, curved or square), diffusion (which determines how much liveliness the walls add to the sound by making the reverb decay more dense) and color (which visually changes the effect from bright to dark).

Compression

The following definitions were created by Dave Kowal for our online classes in Logic and Cubase:

Compression: Affects the dynamic range of a sound by leveling out all the parts so that they don't dynamically jump up and down. There are five basic controls: attack and release, threshold, ratio, and gain.

Attack and Release: A good general approach is to start with the attack time around 1 ms (millisecond) and the release time between 1/2 a second and 1 second. Techniques for specific applications will be discussed as we go.

Threshold: The level of the input signal where the compressor kicks in. You should have 3dB to 6dB of reduction at the strongest point of the track, and there should be times when there's no gain reduction.

Ratio: This ratio is the input level/output level. For example, let's say the ratio is set to 2:1. This means that the output is halved. If it's set at 3:1, only 1/3 of the signal is output. The most natural sounding compression typically has a ratio of 3:1 and 7:1.

Gain: turns up the volume of the entire signal whether it's compressed or not.

Soft Knee/Hard Knee

Two other terms you should know are Soft Knee and Hard Knee. Quoting TC Works, "Soft Knee compression ensures a soft and gradual transition into compression. Hard Knee compression on the other hand, as the name suggests, immediately starts compressing at the maximum level once the threshold is passed. Soft Knee smooths the transition into compression by actually starting to process slightly before the threshold is reached."

I admit, reading this is very confusing. So what you do is record yourself reading a short paragraph, then record a short instrumental with one instrument. Next apply the compressor to hear how the sound changes. Begin working with each control. Hopefully, your system has several compressor presets to work with. If it does, start there.

To illustrate, I've chosen the DeX from TC Works Native Bundle.

Delay

Delays are most often used to set up rhythmic effects.

These controls affect how the delays work:

Feedback - selectively repeats the delayed sound as many times as you choose. A shorter feedback time plays back the sound a fewer number of times. A longer feedback time constantly plays back the sound over and over again.

Mix - this control adjusts the amount of dry signal to the amount of delayed signal. A lower percentage setting only adds a slight amount of delay. A higher percentage setting adds more delay.

Delay - this control selects how long you want the delay to be. A few milliseconds (ms) gives a doubling type of effect, while 500ms (that's a half a second!) will delay the signal by that amount.

To summarize, with delay, you're making time changes of a recorded sound. The more feedback you use and the more delay you use, the more your sound will be placed in a different place in time with the rest of your music.

To illustrate, here's the Stereo Delay from Emagic Logic 4.0.

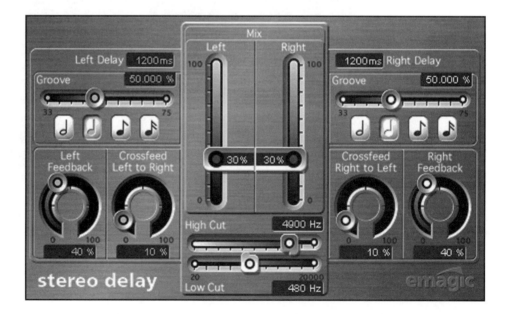

EQ/Equalization

EQ affects the tonal characteristics of a sound by letting you select a frequency (or frequency range) and adjusting the gain (volume!) of that frequency up (boost) or down (cut).

Frequency and Pitch

If I play the note A above middle C on the piano, that's called A3 MIDI language. In engineering language it's called A440, or 440Hz. A4 would be A880 (the frequency doubles as you go up the octaves, halves as you go down). A5 is A1760, or 1.76kHz. Going down, A2 would be A220. A1 is A110 and A0 is A55.

A5 - 1.76 kHz

A4 - 880 Hz

A3 - 440 Hz

A2 - 220 Hz

A1 - 110 Hz

A0 - 55 Hz

EQ Ranges

There are three broad EQ ranges: Lows, Mids, Highs.

1. Highs - above 3.5 kHz

2. Mids - Between 250 Hz to 3.6kHz

3. Lows - below 250 Hz

These are often broken down into 6 specific categories:

- Brilliance: above 6 kHz

- Presence: 3.5kHz - 6 kHz

- Upper Midrange: 1.5kHz to 3.5kHz

- Lower Midrange: 250Hz to 1.5 kHz

- Bass: 60 Hz to 250 Hz

- Sub Bass: below 60 Hz

If we were to translate frequencies into pitches, you'd have a musical range chart. So what EQ does is boost or cut certain frequencies, or range of frequencies, to make an instrument sound more life-like (especially a sample!), or more bright, etc.

Parametric EQ Controls

This EQ plug-in is called a parametric EQ. It has the ability to alter the sound by:

a) Picking the sound area to affect by choosing what's called the CENTER FREQUENCY. This control is constantly variable across a frequency range of 20hz (very low tones) to 20Khz (very high tones).

b) Adjusting how much of that frequency to apply using what's called the q-factor. The q-factor determines over what octave range the frequency will be spread.

c) The GAIN (volume!) control determines how much of the selected frequency to increase or decrease.

To summarize, with EQ, you're making volume (gain) changes to a specific frequency. When it the volume goes up, it's called a boost. When the volume/gain for that frequency goes down, it's called cut.

Here's an example of the TC Works 7-band Parametric EQ.

Where to start

The best way to organize your learning is to start with reverb to hear how it sounds and how to run it into your boards.

Next, I'd work with compression, followed by delays.

Finally, EQ. Now, when it comes to EQ, you should realize that most engineers don't touch EQ until the final part of the mix and the effects have been added. Once the effects have been added, and you hear the brightness and darkness of the whole piece, then you go back and EQ.

What I've covered very briefly in one chapter is really three semesters worth of work. That's because everything here is aural. You have to hear and apply. Alexander University is developing three courses starting with Recording and Reverb, followed by Recording and Effects, and EQ and the Mix that covers this in detail.

Approaching the Final Mix

How you approach the final mix depends directly on the kind of music you're recording, what you're using to record it, how you're recording it, where you're recording it, and the quality of the musical arrangement (regardless of style). Recognize that your procedures for recording and doing the mix are dependent on

- The facility you're recording in

- The musical style

- The approach

- The recorder

- The caliber of the musicians

The broad steps are:

1. Making sure that the musical arrangement of your work is solid

2. Making sure that the performance of your musical work is excellent, non-mechanical and error-free musically

3. Making sure that the arrangement breathes with dynamic changes and occassional time/tempo changes to make it interesting to hear

4. Making sure that the instruments and voices are panned so that everyone has their own "space" and isn't jammed into the center

5. Judicious use of reverb so that everyone is in the same "room"

6. Judicious use of effects to enhance the music without calling undue attention to itself

What you must decide is where these points are being implemented. Are you setting up the mix at a hardware board and then recording the final result as a stereo pair? Are you going to mix inside the computer? Are you mixing inside a digital audio recorder or 4-track?

The point of all these questions is that where you do your mixing determines how you'll automate your mix. If you're doing orchestral work like I do, your mix is done in the computer so that the final version is recorded as either a stereo pair or in 8 tracks (or more, depending on the project) for more specialized EQ and reverb.

Making a tape or CD

Ten years ago, this was a complex task. Today, you do your recording in your digital unit or computer, run the audio outs from the mixing board to a cassette desk, and voila! You have a tape. If you have a DAT machine, you can connect the S/PDIF outs of the audio card to the DAT machine and record direct to DAT.

If you're recording inside a software program, you do a procedure called bounce down that merges all your audio tracks into a single stereo pair. Saved as a .wav file (or aiff on the Mac), you export it to a folder, and using at the very minimum, Adaptec Easy CD Creator, you burn the CD in your computer. Or, you can use the CD burner in your digital audio recorder, or the CD burning feature in Samplitude or Sound Forge.

If you're using a 4-track or a digital recorder with a limited number of audio tracks, bounce down is done to free up tracks. In a computer, if it's set up correctly, you can get 24 or more audio tracks.

For those starting out

My advice is KISS - Keep It Simple Student, and work with a small number of tracks in the beginning.

Conclusion

If you've learned the operations of your tape unit, or gone through our books on the Roland VS1680, Cakewalk, Cubase or Emagic, you now have the basics down for understanding the operations of the software and the mechanics of recording and doing a mix. By applying what you've learned here, you're well on your way to earning your first Grammy. Remember me in your acceptance speech.

Peter Lawrence Alexander

Connecting to a Patchbay

The purpose of an audio patchbay is to let you permanently connect all the inputs and outputs of your audio equipment that you otherwise find yourself repatching while mixing and recording your music. Once all your equipment is plugged into the back of the audio patchbay, short patch cables are then used on the front of the unit to route the signals wherever you want them to go. With a patchbay there's no need to make an Amazonian trek through the forest of wires, man-eating spiders, and other unmentionables lurking at the back of your equipment (and that's for those lucky enough to be able to get back there in the first place.) Once everything's hooked up to the patchbay, all your audio connections are right there in front of you, within arm's reach of the comfort of your chair.

Take a look at the patchbay from Hosa on the following page. You'll see it has two rows of jacks on both the front and the back. It's standard studio practice to use the top row for your outputs and the bottom row for your inputs. It helps to think of these jacks in vertical pairs, you'll understand why as you read on.

See illustration on next page...

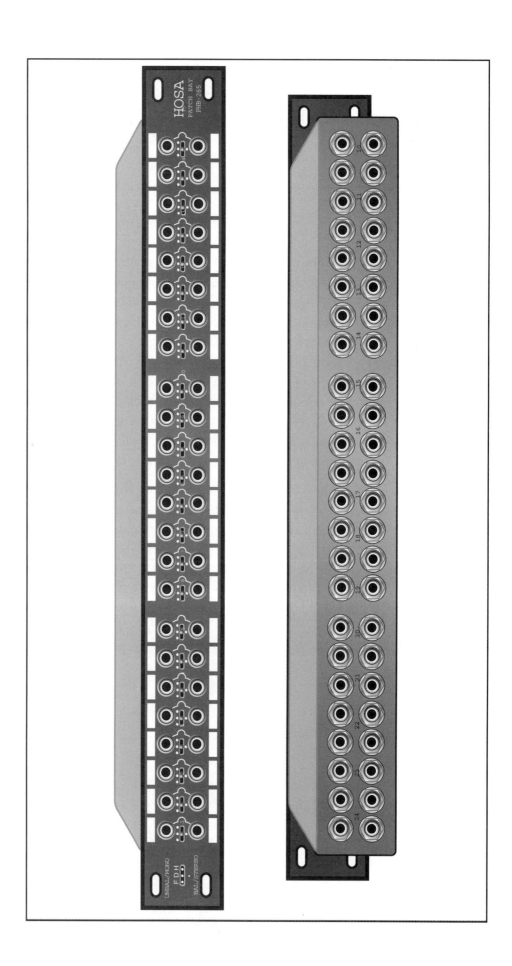

Patchbay back panel connections

Here's a simple setup. The top row of the patchbay has the audio outs from the MIDI equipment. The bottom row is connected to the Mic/Line In of the mixing board.

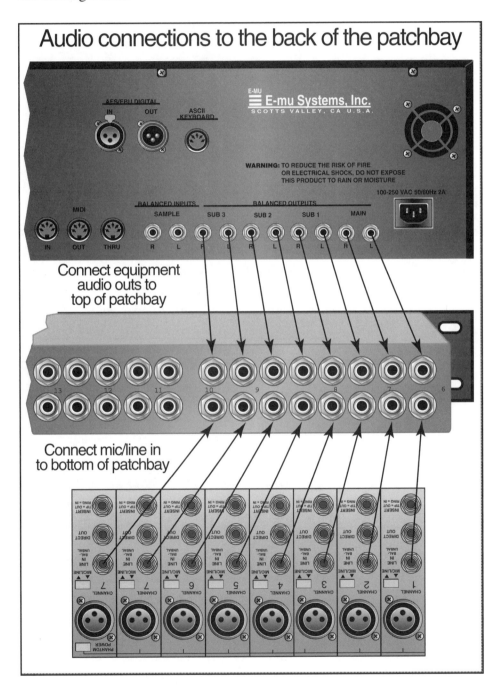

Audio connections to the back of the patchbay

Connect equipment audio outs to top of patchbay

Connect mic/line in to bottom of patchbay

When using a patchbay, you'll hear these three terms that relate to the way the signal flow is routed:

1. Normalled (Full-Normalled)
2. De-Normalled (Non-Normalled/Open)
3. Half-Normalled

Normalled

In a normalled connection, what you assign in the top row is automatically connected to the bottom row. So, looking at the diagram on the previous page, if positions 1-8 on the top row of the patchbay are the audio outs of the E4, positions 1-8 on the mixing board are also the E4. Now, let's say I have an older Roland SP700 with another 8 audio outs that would go to positions 9-16 on the patchbay and match faders 9-16 on the mixing board.

If I want to lay out a string section across the mixing board in the order of the strings, I can use patch cables to break the direct connection of vertical out to in. So if the channel faders 1-4 are violins on the E4, using patch cables I could make channel faders 5 and 6 pizzicato violins from the SP700 with channel faders 7 and 8 being violas from the SP700.

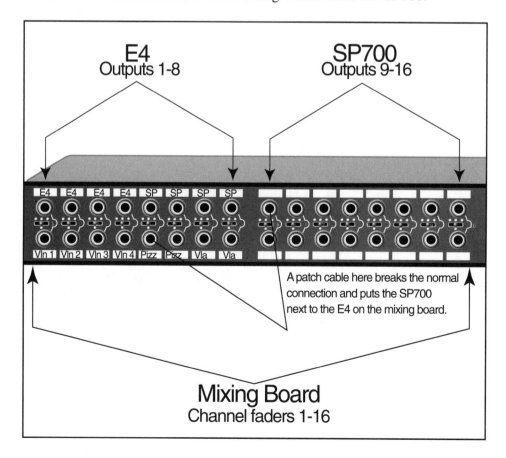

Understanding the connections

When there are no patch cables plugged into the front of the patchbay, the output jack at the back of the patchbay is automatically routed to the input jack immediately below it.

On the front of the patchbay, we connected a 1/4" TS patch cable from Out 9 to In 5. Now take a second 1/4" TS patch cable and repeat for the rest of the connections: Out 10 to In 6, Out 11 to In 7, Out 12 to In 8, etc.

This now breaks the normal internal connection.

Application with Effects

We can do the same thing with effects that we did with MIDI gear. This time connect several effects units in the same position as the E4 in the diagram. On the bottom row, connect the aux returns of the mixing board. You can only have as many aux returns as you have on the mixing board. With this approach you can quickly route effects with minimum fuss.

In the following diagram we've connected a Korg A3 into outputs 1 and 2 on the back of the patchbay. Next to it is a compressor. The aux returns of the board are connected to inputs 1 and 2 directly below. By using the patch cables you've now patched the compressor into the aux returns instead of a channel strip.

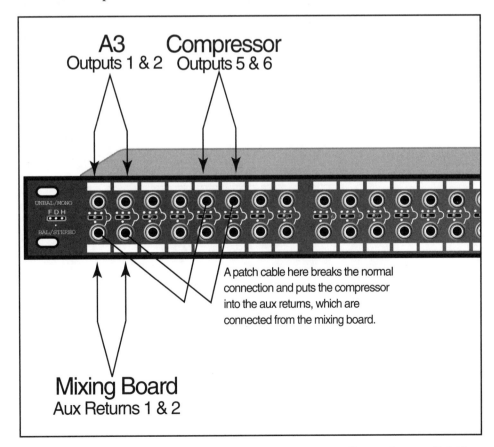

De-Normalled

In a De-Normalled setup every connection must be made with a patch cable. That's because a De-Normalled configuration breaks the vertical pair relationship seen in the Normalled and Half-Normalled configurations. Instead, the audio signal from the back output jack is sent directly to the front output jack, and signal from the back input jack is sent directly to the front input jack. The top and bottom jacks have no internal connection without a patch cable. Look at the diagram below.

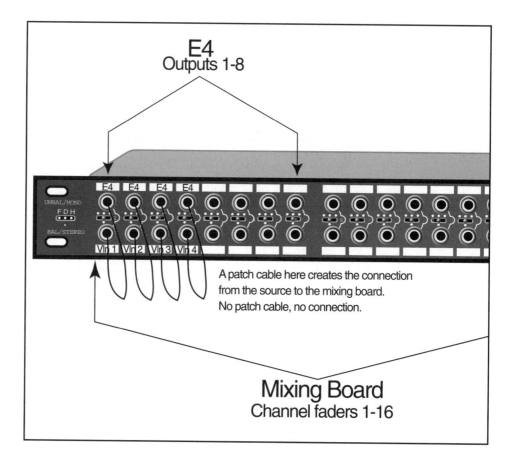

E4
Outputs 1-8

A patch cable here creates the connection from the source to the mixing board. No patch cable, no connection.

Mixing Board
Channel faders 1-16

Half-Normalled

Using the patchbay in a Half-Normalled configuration works in a similar way to the Normalled mode, but lets you route one signal to two different places. Look at the diagram below.

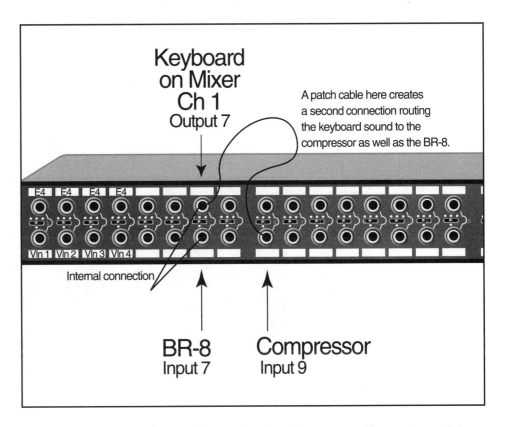

Let's say, for example, you have a keyboard connected in to channel 1 on your mixing board. Now take the output from channel 1 on the board and connect it to an output on the back of the patchbay, we're using Out 7 in the diagram above. Directly below, connected to In 7, we have the Roland BR-8 digital recorder. As with the Normalled configuration, the output of the mixer is automatically routed to the input of the BR-8 directly below it.

Now take a 1/4" TS patch cable and, on the front of the patchbay, connect it from Out 7 to In 9. On the back of the patchbay there's a compressor connected at In 9 and this is where we want to route a second signal to. In Half-Normalled mode, doing this does not break the signal flow between the mixer output and the BR-8. Instead, it takes a *copy* of the output signal from the mixer and routes it to the compressor, so you can process this second signal separately.

The Hosa PHB-265

For this chapter we were provided with the Hosa PHB-265 patch bay, which is designed with Normalled, De-Normalled and Half-Normalled available in any module by simply moving a slider.

There are three positions. To the far left is Full-Normalled, in the middle is De-Normalled, and to the far right is Half-Normalled. See diagram below.

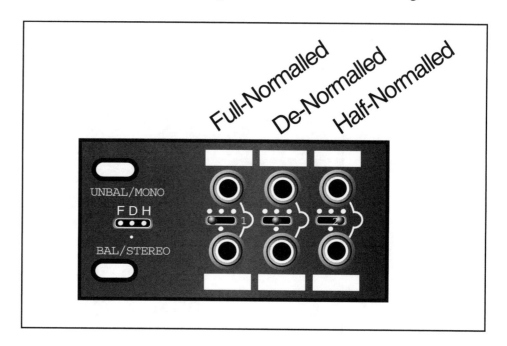

Shure Performance & Recording Microphone Selection Guide

Performance Vocal (Dynamic)

Beta 58A

SM58

Beta 57A

SM57

BG3.1

BG2.1

BG1.1

Studio Vocal

KSM 44

KSM 32

SM81

SM7A

Beta 87A

Beta 87C

SM87A

BG5.1

Performance Vocal (Condenser)

Beta 87A

Beta 87C

SM87A

BG5.1

Ensemble Vocal

KSM 44

KSM 32

SM81

SM94

BG4.1

Headworn Vocal

WCM 16

WH20 XLR

SM10A

SM12A

512

Guitar Amp

Beta 56

Beta 57A

SM57

BG6.1

BG3.1

BG2.1

Bass Amp

Beta 52

SM7A

Beta 57A

Beta 56

SM57

Kick Drum

Beta 52

Beta 91

Beta 57A

SM57

BG6.1

Snare Drum

Beta 57A

Beta 56

SM57

BG6.1

Toms
(Rack & Floor)

Beta 98 D/S

Beta 57A

Beta 56

SM57

BG6.1

Overhead
Cymbals
& Hihat

KSM 44

KSM 32

SM81

SM94

BG4.1

Conga

Beta 98 D/S

Beta 56

Beta 57A

SM57

Mallet
Instruments

KSM 44

KSM 32

SM81

SM91

BG4.1

Marimba &
Other Percussion

KSM 44

KSM 32

SM81

Beta 57A

SM57

Piano

KSM 44

KSM 32

SM81

Beta 91

BG4.1

Strings

KSM 44

KSM 32

SM81

SM94

Beta 98/S

BG4.1

SM11

Acoustic Bass

KSM 44

KSM 32

Beta 52

SM81

SM94

BG4.1

Brass
Instruments

KSM 44

KSM 32

Beta 98/S

Beta 56

Beta 57A

SM57

Woodwinds

KSM 44

KSM 32

SM81

Beta 98/S

BG4.1

Saxophone

KSM 44

KSM 32

Beta 98/S

SM7A

Beta 56

Beat 57A

SM57

Acoustic Guitar

KSM 44

KSM 32

SM81

SM94

BG4.1

Beta 57A

SM57

SM11

Harmonica

520DX "Green Bullet"

SM57

SM58

Leslie Speaker

KSM 44

KSM 32

Beta 57A

Beta 56

Beta 91

SM57

BG3.1

Orchestra

(note 2)

KSM 44

KSM 32

SM81

SM94

BG4.1

Live Recording

(in pairs)

KSM 44

KSM 32

SM81

SM94

BG4.1

VP88 (M-S Stereo)

Stereo Pickup/Ambience

KSM 44

KSM 32

SM81

SM94

BG4.1

VP88 (M-S Stereo)

Sampling

KSM 44

KSM 32

SM81

SM94

BG4.1